IN VINO VERITAS

A BOOK ABOUT WINE

EDITED BY

ANDRÉ L. SIMON

LONDON
GRANT RICHARDS LTD.
MDCCCCXIII

Printing Statement:

Due to the very old age and scarcity of this book,
many of the pages may be hard to read due to the
blurring of the original text, possible missing pages,
missing text, dark backgrounds and other issues
beyond our control.

Because this is such an important and rare work, we
believe it is best to reproduce this book regardless of
its original condition.

Thank you for your understanding.

CONTENTS

INTRODUCTION

Addressing a meeting of total abstainers, at Manchester, a short time ago, the Bishop of Lincoln deplored the fact that teetotalism was making no headway. The common sense of the race is asserting itself and condemns with equal justice all excesses ; intemperance in drink is universally deprecated and the intemperance in speech and statement of total abstinence advocates, " whose antagonism to alcohol has fossilised into superstition," is equally condemned by all sober-minded people.

The immense majority of brain-workers, in this as in all other civilised countries, drink wines and spirits, and there must be many who would like to know something more reliable about alcohol than what is to be found in the numerous publications issued by total abstinence associations. There has not been any comprehensive work upon wines and spirits published in England for many years, and the Committee of the Wine Trade Club have decided to issue a series of text-books to supply the public as well as wine-merchants with authentic facts and figures about wines and spirits.

The present volume is the first of these text-books ; it consists of six chapters which correspond to the six lectures delivered by the Wine Trade Club at Vintners' Hall during the winter of 1911—1912. It may be said to form an introduction to the study of the subject ; it contains a strictly correct but very short description of the history of the wine trade in England and general information on the growing of vines, the art of wine-making, the science of distillation and the effects of alcohol upon the human body. Some will be satisfied with the superficial knowledge gained from the following pages, but many more may be induced thereby to take a keener interest than hitherto into a branch of commerce the study of which offers a larger and more varied field of research than any other.

The next volumes will deal exhaustively with the different wines of the world at the historical and technical points of

view. One volume of the series will deal
with the botanical, scientific, chemical,
medical, and political aspects of the question, whilst another volume will be entirely
devoted to spirits.

A. L. S.

Christmas, 1912.

CHAPTER I

The Wine Trade of England
Past and Present

THERE is no trade in the land of greater antiquity than the Wine Trade, nor can any other branch of commerce claim to possess greater or wider interest.

The Romans, during their occupation of Britain, probably imported some wine for their own use, but they never introduced viticulture in the country, nor can they be said to have established a regular trade in wines between England and the Continent.

The use of wine and the knowledge of

viticulture in England are coeval with the introduction of the Christian faith.

In nearly every Eastern and Continental province of the Roman Empire, vines were 'cultivated and wine was easy to procure ; not so, however, in Britain, and there is no doubt that wine was imported regularly by the first Christian priests who obtained a sufficiently secure footing in this country and were able to build a church or monastery as a permanent abode.

These early missionaries kept as close a connection as the times permitted with the larger and wealthier churches already flourishing in Gaul ; they were, in many instances, the offshoots of these Continental missions, which supplied them with the clothing and the wine necessary to carry on their ministry, as well as with spiritual guidance.

The Christian priests were more than mere religious teachers ; they were " the agents through whom the English came into real contact with the heritage of civilised life which had survived the destruction of the Roman Empire." *

---

* W. Cunningham, *The Growth of English Industry and Commerce during the Early and Middle Ages.*

Their influence on the social and commercial life of Britain, whose inhabitants " were steeped in the squalor of unintelligent poverty,"* was far more considerable than that of the Romans, whilst the constant intercommunications of British and Continental religious houses served to encourage the development of foreign trade.

Wine was imported into England during the fifth century, since it was served at the feast given by Hengist to Vortigern, when Rowena, who was soon to become the British chief's bride, drank his health in a golden bowl " filled with wine."

In the following century, the fact that the princely Murchertach, son of Erc, fell and was drowned in a butt of wine, is vouched for by the learned editor of the Tripartite Life of St. Patrick, in the annals from the Book of Leinster.

There is, however, very little doubt that the foreign trade of England, such as it was, was practically annihilated when the Saxons obtained the mastery of the

---

* Coote, *Romans of Britain.*

northern seas, desolated the coasts of England and, by degrees, conquered almost the whole of the land. Under their heathen conquerors, the inhabitants of Britain relapsed into comparative barbarism, and every trace of former religion and commerce disappeared from these islands.

When, however, the conquest of the bulk of Britain had been completed by the Saxons, the older wars of extermination came to an end; the new settlers realised the folly of ruthless destruction, and agriculture, trade and progress received more attention. Commerce, unfortunately, was perforcedly limited on account of the insecurity of the roads and the difficulty of developing the internal trade of the country. It was not before the reign of Alfred that the internal and foreign trade of England was placed on a sound basis, by the creation of taxes and customs which rendered the position of the foreign trader definite whilst his obligations were limited and became precise. Some sixty years later, during the reign of Edgar (A.D. 957–975) and the wise government of Dunstan, the commerce of England reached a degree of prosperity it had never attained before.

It is from that time onwards that we find documentary proofs of the magnitude as well as of the antiquity of the English wine trade.

Rouen enjoyed during the tenth and eleventh centuries a monopoly of the trade in French wines sent abroad from the interior, by the Seine. The navigation of the lower Seine, from Rouen to the Channel, was free to citizens of the metropolis of Normandy, and all the export trade of French wines to England was in their hands. The privileges they had in Dunstan's time were amplified by Ethelred II. and by his son, Edward the Confessor, who had been educated in Normandy, where he lived twenty-seven years. The traders of Rouen had a special port of their own, called Dunegate, in London ; whilst the Germans, who, according to Heyd, came probably from the fair at Frankfort-on-Main and from Mainz, were already established in London in a permanent position in the reign of Ethelred, their privileges being carefully noted in the laws of this prince.

It is a well-known fact that, as soon
as a special article of food or material of
manufacture became the object of larger
importation in England, special duties
were immediately imposed on such articles
or materials in the hope of deriving greater
profit from the increasing demand. It is,
therefore, worthy of notice that wine was
one of the very first articles on which
a special tax was levied, which proves
that the wine trade, at the close of the
tenth century, had already acquired some
importance in England.

During the reign of Ethelred II., it was
ordained that the men of Rouen who
came with wine, were to pay " the right
toll of six shillings for a large ship. . . ."
There is every reason to believe that what
is termed the right toll of six shillings per
large ship of wine was not a new tax, and
that it had been established in some previous reign, although there are no records
extant showing this to have been the
case.

To supply the demand for wine, which
had already become considerable before
the Norman Conquest, a large number of

men were employed in importing this
commodity into England and in retailing
it. It is absolutely certain that both
wholesale and retail wine merchants were
trading in this country before the middle
of the eleventh century. Edward the
Confessor, in spite of his goodwill for the
men of Rouen to whom he granted many
privileges, and whilst professing to be anxious
to facilitate their trade in wines with this
country, decreed that foreigners could
only sell their wines wholesale in England,
and that they were not to cause any prejudice to the native Englishmen by taking
up the retail trade or engaging in any
work which the citizens were wont to do.

The importance of the Norman Conquest and its influence upon the commercial
life of England cannot be exaggerated.
To use Miss Bateson's original metaphor,
England, during the reigns of the Norman
kings, " was swept out of its backwater
into the main stream of Continental civili-
zation."

William of Normandy and his followers,
noblemen, gentlemen, and others who
shared the spoils of victory, were all wine

drinkers. At the same time, the much
greater security of the Channel and the
inducements given to French traders to
come and settle in England, all tended
to greatly improve the trade in wine
between England and the Continent.

The abundance of wine in England
during the twelfth century was such that,
even during the troubled reign of Stephen,
the king could fine an offending lord,
Matthew de Vernum, in a hundred casks
of wine for a breach of the peace.

There is also an order of his predecessor,
Henry I., who, in 1130, instructed Milo
de Gloucester, sheriff of Shropshire, to
send a quantity of wine to Worcester and
Bridgnorth.

A minute account of Henry I.'s expenses, which has come down to us, shows
that this monarch required very large
quantities of wine. In the king's household, many officers, stallers, marshals,
chamberlains, and officers of all sorts were
in receipt of bread and wine for their
private consumption. This was called
the "livery," the recipients of which
ranked from the High Court officials in

London and Winchester down to the watch, the porter and the servants of St. Briavel's Castle, in Gloucestershire.

Ever since the latter part of the eleventh century until the Revolution of 1688, it was customary for the servants and officers of the royal palaces and residences through- out the land to be supplied with wine by the monarch. Moreover, all the royal castles on the coast of England, on the Marches of Wales or on the Scottish Bor- der, received wine from the king for the use of the lord in command and of his men. This supply was even so plentiful that it is recorded that during the siege of Exeter, the water supply having failed, wine had to be used to make bread and to put out firebrands.

The numerous claims on the Royal Exchequer would never have permitted the sovereign to buy the enormous quan- tities of wine he stood in need of ; most of this was obtained from the " prisage " or " recta prisa," which consisted in the king's right to take from each cargo of wine arriving in England, one cask on each side the mast, unfranked. If this were not sufficient to furnish the required quantity of wine, part of the cargo was purchased in the king's name, at about half the price then ruling ; if more than this were wanted, and it happened by no means unfrequently, the ship with all its cargo was chartered by the Crown and navigated forthwith to the port nearest to the ultimate destination of the wine. It seems, however, to have been usual to subject none but foreign vessels to this arbitrary measure.

The prisage had originated in free gifts of wine to the king by foreign merchant-vintners in return for the protection they were accorded when trading in England, until it came to be recognised as a custom or royal due. The right of the sovereign to buy at his own price the necessaries of life, bread and wine, required by his household and his army, was also sub-mitted to as a national royal prerogative ; " ad opus regis et suorum " was a formula which opened every warehouse and every cellar, the king's claims being always paramount.

The Patent Rolls and the Close Rolls

contain a great many entries relating to
the number of casks of wine the kings
received as prisage, for over six centuries,
from the wine-laden ships which reached
London, Southampton, Sandwich, Chester,
Bristol, Boston and other ports. These
entries prove beyond a doubt that the
wine trade of England was one of the
most active and one of the most con-
sistently important branches of our commerce during the twelfth and the following
three centuries.

Wine was, then, mostly consumed the
year after the vintage, and sold at very
low prices.   Only noblemen and rich
commoners, who possessed an ample in-
come, were allowed to import wine or to
buy it wholesale.   Traders, clerks, farmers,
artisans and others had to buy wine at
the taverns, where it was retailed at prices
fixed by authority, and for consumption
either off or on the premises.

As a rule, taverners do not appear to
have possessed sufficient capital to buy
more than a few casks of wine direct
from the importers; they had to purchase most of what they required from

native vintners, many of whom were
wealthy men. It was not unusual for
vintners to stock the cellars of taverners
who were unable to buy their wine out-
right, and who were practically in the
same position as the tenants of the present
day tied houses. On August 16th, 1281,
for instance, Christian the Taverner ac-
knowledged having received six casks of
wine, value £13, from William Varache,
for sale, together with four silver cups,
which he would account for when he had
sold the wine ; and for so doing he pledged
himself and chattels.

It is permissible to infer that taverners
were often bound in some way to the
vintners, from the opening sentence of
Edward III.'s ordinance of November
8th, 1327, against the mixing of weak and
bad wine with any other, which the king
had been given to understand was practised by the vintners of the City of
London and *their* taverners selling wine by
retail.

Both the vintners and taverners, particularly the latter, were hampered by
many legislative restrictions before they

could dispose of the wines they had bought. In London, the municipal authorities were more meddlesome than in any other city or town, and interfered to a very considerable extent with the trade of the taverners, apparently on account of a jealous care of the citizens' health.

Jurors were appointed to search all the tavern cellars in the City, and to examine the wines sold thereat, and Edward III. even ordered that the wine that was in cellars and in taverns should be examined by the Lord Mayor, who was to see that putrid and bad wines were destroyed.

Each customer had a right to see his wine drawn and could go to the cellar and see the cask whence it was drawn; the taverner was not even allowed to have a cloth before the door of his cellar, so that everyone could see what was going on. The mixing or blending of new with old wine was not only forbidden, but the two were not even allowed to be kept in the same place; all the old wine which might remain having to be removed to some other place before a taverner could lodge new wine in his cellar, and none of

B

this was allowed to be sold before all the old wine had been disposed of.

The same prohibition applied to different sorts of wine sold at a tavern; the white wines of Gascony, Rochelle or Spain were not to be put in the same cellar where Rhenish wine was kept, and, when sweet wines were allowed to be sold, no other kind was to be kept in the same tavern.

The object of these enactments was to prevent dealers in wine fraudulently substituting one wine for another, and very severe penalties were incurred by taverners selling a wine for what it was not; similar ordinances had in view the selling of the right quantity paid for by the consumer, and taverners were ordered to sell all their wines in standard measures sealed by the sheriffs and aldermen, and never by the cruskyn, or cruse, a small earthenware cup from which the wine was drunk.

The many ordinances and regulations devised to protect the public from unscrupulous traders and the merchants from unfair competition, could never have been enforced with any success had it not

been for the influence and work of a power-
ful guild, one of the twelve Great Livery
Companies, the Worshipful Company of
Vintners.

Early in the fourteenth century, during
the reign of Edward II., the Bordeaux
wine merchants trading with England
formed themselves into a confederation
for the greater security and better regula-
tion of their trade. They were commonly
called the *Merchant-Wine-Tonners of Gas-
coyne*, but did not form a sanctioned or
articled Company. Their agreements were
purely private; to some was entrusted
the care of recovering all moneys remaining due after the departure of the sellers;
to others was confided the charge of obtaining from the King's Council advan-
tageous privileges or the renewal of these
at the accession of every new monarch,
all the expenses thus incurred being shared
equally by all the merchants. Many of
these men, chosen by their fellows for
their energy and intelligence, attained high
distinction in England, where they were
not considered as foreigners, being Gascon
subjects of the king.

Thus, William Trente, a native of Bergerac, became the King's Butler and Chamberlain of the City in the reign of Edward I., whilst John Adrian, Henry Picard, and several others, became Mayors of London, during Edward III.'s reign.

The Merchant-Wine-Tonners of Gascoigne were originally divided into two classes: the importers and retailers, *Vinetarii* and *Tabernarii*, the former selling their wine wholesale or leaving it to the tabernarii or retailers to dispose of it for their account. But this did not last long, as the London municipal authorities forced the Gascons to submit to their regulations, excluding all but citizens of London from the right to sell wine by retail in London and the liberties thereof. After an unsuccessful attempt to assert their own privileges against those of the City, the Gascons arrived at a friendly working arrangement with the Londoners by the formation of an association of London Vintners, comprising Londoners and Gascons having obtained the freedom of the City. The importing vintners were sacrificed chiefly owing to the rapid growth

of the Flemish and Genoese merchant
shipping, to which so large a share of the
carrying trade was soon to fall. The
resident vintners still retained the former
distinction of *vinetarii*, those who sold
wholesale or financed retailers, and the
tabernarii, or retailers who kept a tavern
or a cellar of their own, or on some vintner's account.

Articles of association and letters of
incorporation are not in existence to show
that the vintners had thus organised
themselves in London in the earlier part
of the fourteenth century for the better
defence of their rights against the preten-
sions of a grasping Corporation, and for
the more profitable prosecution of their
trade ; but other documents exist which
prove beyond a doubt the existence of a
well-defined organisation known in 1328,
if not before, as the Mistery of the Vintners. In that year (2 Edward III.), we
find in the Letter Books of the City of
London the names of many Vintners
amongst those elected and sworn in divers
misteries of London, for the government
and instruction of their craft.

Three years later, in 1331, the names of the Vintners recorded at the Guildhall were more numerous still, and included some "taverners" for the first time.

It was not, however, until July 15th, 1364, that the Vintners obtained royal letters patent forbidding anyone meddling with their trade "unless enfranchised in the Mistery." This charter, entitled "Ample Liberties for the Vintners of London," did not merely regulate their trade, as alleged by Strype, who in this contradicts Stow; "it is as much an incorporation charter as any granted to the other great Livery Companies at the time."

It practically gave the London Vintners the monopoly of the retail trade in the metropolis, as far as Gascon wines were concerned ; the Gascons were forbidden to sell the wine they imported, otherwise than wholesale, by the tun or pipe. By this charter, the members of the Vintners' Company were invested with the right of trade search to ascertain whether the wines offered for sale within the City were sound and wholesome. They were to choose, each year, four of their members, amongst those who did not keep a tavern, to be presented to and sworn before the Lord Mayor, and in them was vested a very considerable authority ; these four experts not only advised the municipal authorities as to the price at which wine was to be retailed in taverns, but they were empowered to correct and amend defaults they detected in the exercise of the craft, and to inflict fines according to their good advice or judgment.

The jurisdiction and influence which the members of the Vintners' Company came to enjoy as a result of this charter were very considerable, but they do not appear to have been abused, since most of its provisions were either renewed or amplified in 1370, in 1377 and at later dates.

In 1422, a royal ordinance, which was confirmed in 1427, received the assent of Parliament, and was practically a repetition of the Statute of 37 Edward III., cap. 5. It enacted that " no Englishman shall go to Gascony or elsewhere to buy wine or bring it to England unless he be free of the mistery of the vintry in London, or be experienced in the mistery, and known to be of it, in

other cities, boroughs or towns. Merchants
of Gascony and other foreigners may bring
wine to England, but may not sell it by
retail there ; no private person or stranger,
after having brought wine to England, may
export it again without special leave of the
king. The said merchants of the mistery
of the merchandize of wine are to elect
yearly four of their number, not being
tavern keepers, to survey the trade in
London, and in each town where the mistery is used. Wine must be landed above
London Bridge, at the Vintry, for the con-
venience of the king's butler, gauger and
searchers, etc."

It was only ten years later, on August
23rd, 1437, that the Mistery of Vintners
of London was formally incorporated, re-
ceiving the ordinary privileges and en-
dowments as to perpetual succession, the
right of using a common seal and of plead-
ing and being impleaded in all courts, the
title to appoint a governing body of four
masters or wardens, and a licence in mort-
main to the extent of £20 a year. This
incorporation was followed, in 1447, by
the grant of arms to the Mistery.

The power and influence of the Vintners'
Company in London had been gradually
rising during the fourteenth century; in
the earlier part of the fifteenth century
this progress was stopped, and unmistak-
able signs of decadence made their appearance some fifty years later.

It must not be forgotten that the privileges and rights granted to the freemen
of the Mistery of Vintners were limited
to the trade in Gascon wines.

The sale of German, Levant or Spanish
wines was regulated by special ordinances,
and according to certain treaties of recipro-
city entered into between England and
Flanders, Spain or Venice. Both the royal
and municipal authorities had always carefully kept the sale of German and of sweet
wines outside the pale of the Vintners'
jurisdiction. Thus, in 1369, Edward III.
ordered formally that Rhenish wine should
not be kept in the same taverns as Gascon
white wine, so that the searchers appointed
by the Vintners could not interfere; a
similar prohibition, respecting the sale of
sweet wines, had been issued as far back as
1353. In 1365, the London municipality

took into their own hands the retail sale
of sweet wines in a few special taverns
under their own supervision. This attempt,
however, having proved most unsuccessful,
it was agreed to issue licences for the sale
of sweet wines to any freeman of the City,
or even to foreigners, who were ready to
pay for that privilege the price fixed by
the Corporation.

Such licences and the privileges of the
merchants of the Steelyard, who claimed
to have the right of selling Rhenish wine
in London, did not affect the prosperity
and power of the Vintners' Company, so
long as the importance of the Bordeaux
wine trade with England remained paramount, as it had been during the reigns of
Edward III. and his immediate successors ;
but after the loss of Guienne and Gascony,
this branch of the English wine trade,
which had so long eclipsed all others, suffered to a very large extent, whilst other
French wines, as well as German, Spanish
and Levant wines, became more popular.

The Vintners, whose prestige and means
had decreased during the commercial crisis
which followed the loss of the French

provinces and the Wars of the Roses, failed, at first, to secure from Henry VII. a renewal of their ancient privileges. This monarch allowed all his subjects to go to Gascony for wines, and only prohibited the sale of those Bordeaux wines which were imported in foreign bottoms, even if such wines belonged to freemen of the Vintners' Company.

It was not until 1508 that Henry VII. consented to renew the ancient privileges of the Vintners' Company by the grant of an inspeximus of Henry VI.'s charter.

On January 20th, 1530, the most complete ordinance regulating the wine trade in England was issued, covering no less than thirteen full folios of one of the great Letter Books of the Guildhall, in which it is clearly stated that not only freemen of the Vintners' Company, but freemen of all the Livery Companies were free to retail wine in London.

The Vintners' Company made a determined stand to oppose, during the reigns of Edward VI. and of Queen Mary, the inimical legislation directed against them, which dictated the patents of May 22nd

and September 30th, 1553, and of March
26th, 1554. They eventually succeeded
in obtaining, on July 30th, 1558, the grant
of a charter recognising most of their
former privileges. It was not, however,
before November, 1566, that a Bill was
sanctioned repealing the Act of 7 Edward
VI. (1553), and granting full liberty to
the London Vintners to buy and sell wine
wherever they pleased. The Vintners obtained two charters from Queen Elizabeth,
on May 17th, 1567, and on October 12th,
1576, whilst a very important ordinance,
in 1583, fixed and regulated their trade
in its minutest details. Much stress was
laid in this ordinance on the licensing
question; no Vintner was allowed to
keep more than one tavern, and the
magistrates were to see that the number
of such taverns "do not inordinately
exceed" the requirements of the time.
At the same time, the Vintners were entrusted with the duty of watching and
reporting how the Queen's commandments
were kept by all persons selling wine.

During the reigns of Henry VII. and
Henry VIII., all persons were free to retail

wine who had obtained a licence from the municipal authorities, whose duty it was to ascertain that the applicants had served a sufficient term of apprenticeship to be conversant with matters pertaining to the trade they wished to take up. Freemen of the Vintners' Company, however, were not under the necessity of obtaining such a licence, since the first condition of their eligibility to the Company was that they should have been apprenticed to a Vintner and thus learned their trade.

During the latter part of the sixteenth century, licences for retailing wine were also granted directly by the monarch, and, unfortunately, without enforcing the stipulated apprenticeship.

Thus, in 1583, Queen Elizabeth granted licences for the retail of wine in London to two Drapers, one Mercer, two Grocers, nine Merchant-Tailors, four Haberdashers, four Cloth-Workers, three Fishmongers, one Chandler, one Dyer, one Salter, one Cook, two Coopers, two Girdlers, and the widow of a Barber Surgeon.

Elizabeth granted a great many such licences, and although she renewed the

Vintners' Charter in 1567, and again in
1577, she prefaced the latter with a statement which must have been very dis-
tasteful to the Company, to the effect that
everyone was free " to pursue such lawful
calling whereby he may gain his living, as
is most agreeable to his choice or taste."
At the same time, she repeated and amplified a decree of Henry VIII., to the effect
that all freemen of the City of London,
and the widows of such, were free to sell
wine " in London or Westminster, South-
wark, and the liberties of our Duchy of
Lancaster without Temple Bars in London."

The rôle played by the Vintners' Company, whose authority was continually
traversed and curtailed by the grant of
licences to independent persons, became
more and more administrative. Vintners
still helped the municipal authorities carry
into effect royal ordinances fixing the
retail price of wine and, generally speaking, were entrusted by the Corporation
with a large share of the policing of the
wine trade, particularly as regards the
sale of wine in taverns ; but they never
recovered the preponderance which they

had enjoyed at the close of the fourteenth century.

The policy of granting monopolies and of farming royal customs on imports for the sake of immediate revenue, was inaugurated by Elizabeth, and the Stuarts readily adopted it. This system proved not only detrimental to the best interests of the Crown, but also very injurious to commerce in general, and to the wine trade in particular; it was responsible to a great extent for the higher prices demanded for wine, during the seventeenth century, and also for the numerous complaints from all quarters, during the same period, that the quality of the wines sold had greatly deteriorated. Higher prices and poorer quality, even more than civil wars, affected the wine trade of England adversely during the seventeenth century.

It is quite a common error to imagine that during the Revolution and Cromwell's Administration, the wave of puritanism which swept over England greatly checked the consumption of wine. The Roundheads and Puritans of those days were absolutely free from the cant of the bigoted,

self-righteous total abstainer of modern
times. They were men of action as well
as of high ideals, and whilst deprecating
all excesses, they had too much common
sense not to recognise the benefits which
man derived in body and mind from the
temperate use of wine.

In 1650, the attention of the first Commonwealth Parliament having been called
to the greatly increased prices merchants
asked for wine, a Committee was immediately appointed to consider the law as to
setting a price upon wines, and to bring
in a Report to the House " for preventing
the evil now growing by the great price
which is put upon Spanish wines."

Spanish wine, known as Sack, was then
imported in very large quantities and
formed by far the most important branch
of the wine trade of England.

French wines were more costly and not
so generally consumed, but they were not
banished from Whitehall, during Cromwell's
Administration, in spite of the republican
simplicity affected by the Protector, the
plain fare at whose table was the subject
of many a sneer amongst the Royalists.

In 1654, for instance, the Commissioners for prize goods delivered ten tuns of wine for the use of the Protector in January ; in the following March, they delivered five tuns of French wine on one occasion, and forty tuns of French wine, out of the *Hope of Rouen*, a few days later, for His Highness. At that same time, Cromwell purchased a further supply of forty tuns of French wines out of the *St. Katherine of Horn*, as well as forty tuns of French wines from some other source.

There are many such entries in the State Papers showing that the Protector, his officers and household consumed a considerable quantity of wine ; there are also many proofs to be drawn from the same source of the care Cromwell took to keep both the naval and land forces well supplied with wine. It was not only when the Commonwealth's ships called at some port of a wine producing country, nor when some wine-laden vessel was captured at sea, that the fleet were able to have some wine ; Parliament voted regularly large sums for the purchase of sufficient supplies of beverage wines for the men.

The reign of Charles II. marks a period
of great depression for the wine trade.
In 1660, Parliament raised the duty on
wine to £6 per tun, and prohibited the
importation of wine in foreign bottoms.
To make matters worse, all trade and
commerce between England and the
Canary Islands was prohibited in 1666;
the following year, Charles II. also prohibited the importation of all French
goods into England, hoping to thus cripple
France's commerce and force Louis XIV.
to ask for peace. English merchants peti-
tioned the king, praying—but in vain,—
that the said proclamation might be re-
called, saying that " it would very considerably abate the customs, destroy a
great part of the Duke of York's revenue
for wine-licences, and cause French wines
to be brought in as Rhenish." Happily,
the peace of Breda being signed in July
1667, wine was once more allowed to be
imported from France, and such large
quantities were then brought over, that
Parliament considered the state of the
wine trade in England sufficiently flourishing to bear an additional duty of £4 per

tun, which was imposed in 1668. A little later, the duty on all wines was further raised to £12 per tun, and, in 1679, war having broken out once more, the importation of French wines and other goods was again prohibited, a measure which was only repealed in 1685, when James II. ascended the throne.

William III. raised the duties on wine, in 1693, and inaugurated the imposition of a scale of duties on different wines according to their country of origin ; thus, French wine paid £22 2s. 10d. per tun ; Rhenish wine £19 17s. 3d. per tun ; and Spanish and Portuguese wines, £17 13s. 3d. per tun. The same scale was adhered to in 1697, when the duties on French, Rhenish and Peninsular wines were raised to £47 2s. 10d., £26 2s. 10d., and £21 12s. 5d. respectively.

In spite of such excessive duties, and in spite of the heavy taxation necessitated by the prosecution of an expensive war on the Continent, the wine trade remained very active. In giving the detail of the different wines cleared in the port of London, in 1694–5, Houghton remarks that the total is

only about 17,000 tuns, which, he adds,
" is but a small matter considering what
was brought in before the War ; for I have
been told by the City Gauger, that there has
come to London in one year 31,000 tuns of
wine." This would have been equivalent
to 7,812,000 gallons of wine, imported in
London alone, or more than a gallon per
head of the whole population of Great
Britain at that time. This quantity did
not strike Houghton as being excessive,
for he further stated that " 'tis a pity
we do not drink 30 gallons a head. . . . "
What would the worthy man think of
the present generation if he could but
know that the total imports of wine in
the whole of Great Britain and Ireland
are now less than a quarter of a gallon
per head of the population per year ?

The history of the wine trade in England during the eighteenth century is
chiefly remarkable for the rapid decline
in the consumption of French wines, and
the favour which the wines of Portugal
came to enjoy.

When William of Orange ascended the
English Throne, his arch-enemy Louis XIV

was at the zenith of his glory. Louis's
power on the Continent, the hospitality
he accorded to the exiled Stuarts, his treat-
ment of the Huguenots, and Colbert's
commercial policy, were all calculated to
inspire the king and the people of England with feelings of hatred against France
and everything that was French. When
Queen Anne succeeded William III., her
Government knew that any measure likely
to cause serious prejudice to the French
was sure to be immensely popular. They
accordingly sought to ruin one of the
most important and prosperous branches
of France's trade, the trade in wines,
by admitting the wines of Portugal in
England on payment of £7 per tun, whilst
the wines of France were to pay £55 per
tun. This was the object of the famous
Methuen Treaty signed in 1703, which
Anderson calls " a most just and beneficial
Convention," adding that he hoped it
might remain inviolate for ever. Later
historians, however, all agree that the
Methuen Treaty was, on the whole, very
prejudicial to English interests, both commercially and politically. By this treaty,

we gained the Portuguese market for
woollens, but lost the far more important
market of France; worse than this, it
materially contributed to keep England
and France from forming any really cordial
and intimate relations.

Protests were at first loud and numerous: General Churchill, Marlborough's
brother, the rich Pereira, the jovial Port-
man Seymour, Dean Aldrich, " the Apostle
of Bacchus," Doctor Ratcliffe, who ascribed
all diseases to the lack of French wines,
and a host of bottle companions, poets
and satirists, lawyers and physicians, during the reign of Queen Anne, would and
did drink their favourite claret, in spite
of treaties and duties. However exorbit-
ant the charge for French wines, there
was a demand for them so long as the
generation of men lasted who had been
boys in Charles II.'s time, but the generations which followed never had the
opportunity of appreciating the vintages
of France sufficiently to pay the price
demanded for them; their consumption
gradually decreased almost to vanishing
point, and, in that respect, the promoters

of the Methuen Treaty attained the object
they had in view. It was not, however,
solely the increased price at which French
wines had to be sold that lost them the
favour of the vast majority of wine
drinkers in England. The principal cause
is to be found in the ceaseless endeavours
of politicians, divines, satirists and others
to sow and foster throughout the country
a most bigoted hatred of the French
and everything that was French.

What could be expected of the narrow-
minded eighteenth-century country squire
and parson, of the stout self-made Alder-
man in the City, when a man of Swift's
culture and intellect wrote :

> " Be sometimes to your country true,
> Have once the public good in view,
> Bravely despise Champagne at Court,
> And choose to dine at home with Port ! "

These lines, which are poor poetry and
worse reasoning, are but a mild example
of the arguments used on platforms, in
innumerable pamphlets and songs, and
even in the pulpit, to convince the people
of England that the Ship of State must
either float in Port or ignominiously founder

in French wine. However unreasonable
such a proposition appears to us, it was
so diligently and so perseveringly used
during the eighteenth century, that it
was eventually accepted by nearly all
classes of the community as a sound and
profitable argument.

Although the Methuen Treaty crippled
the trade in French wines, it had very
little influence for many years on the
quantity of Portugal wines imported in
England. The trade in wines between our
country and Portugal dates back to the
fourteenth century, and Oporto wines were
known in England during the seventeenth
century. There were 12,465 pipes of wine
exported from Oporto to England, in 1692,
and 13,011 pipes, in 1693, before the
Methuen Treaty was ever thought of;
whilst the average yearly exports from
Oporto to England only reached 8,111
pipes from 1703 till 1712, and the imports
of Portugal wine were smaller in 1730 and
in 1740 than in 1699. But, whilst 8,703
pipes imported in 1699 from Oporto were
equal to 40 per cent. of the total imports,
7,524 pipes imported in 1740 were equal

to about 50 per cent. of the total imports.
In other words the consumption of Port
wine in England did not increase materially for many years after the Methuen
Treaty, but the consumption of French
wines declined so rapidly, that the proportion of Portuguese wines consumed in
England increased from 40 per cent. of
the total, at the close of the seventeenth
century, to 72 per cent., at the close of the
eighteenth century.

During the first half of the eighteenth
century, Port had little to recommend it
but its cheapness, but, during the second
half of the same century, both the price
and the quality of Port were raised gradually, with the result that the popularity
of the wine, as shown by the figures relating to imports, increased steadily until the
superiority of Port over all other wines
became part and parcel of the creed of every
true-born and true-hearted Englishman.

During the first half of the nineteenth
century, the wine trade of England was
in the hands of a comparatively small
number of private wine-merchants, who
obtained their supplies either direct from

abroad or from a few large wholesale
houses in London. The two principal qualities good wine was expected to possess
were colour and sugar. Nobody, then,
would have dared deny that the first
duty of a wine was to be red and its
second to be sweet. Stout, dark vintage
ports were the rule ; full, sweet sherries
and brown Madeiras were their only
competitors in the public favour. Sweet
Champagne was becoming more popular
amongst the wealthy classes, and there
was only a small but regular demand for
the finest hocks and clarets Germany and
France could produce.

Cheap wines were then practically unknown, and cash payments would have been
resented as an insult. A wine-merchant
was expected to be a gentleman possessed
of considerable means and knowledge,
which enabled him to give his customer
long credit and fine quality ; his prices
were no more questioned than the fees of
the physician.

This state of affairs came to an abrupt
end in the sixties when Gladstone revolu-
tionised the wine trade of England.

On February 29th, 1860, the duty on every description of wine was lowered to 3s. per gallon. On January 1st, 1861, this uniform rate was superseded by the imposition of a scale of duties, based on the degrees of strength, according to Sykes's hydrometer, ranging from 1s. per gallon on wines containing less than 18 degrees of alcohol, to 2s. 11d. per gallon on wines containing 45 degrees of alcohol. On April 3rd, 1862, this scale was further revised and lowered, all wines containing less than 26 degrees of alcohol being admitted at the rate of 1s. per gallon, whilst those containing more, up to 42 degrees, were to pay 2s. 6d. per gallon.

Such a drastic reduction in the duties on wine was bound to have an immediate and considerable influence upon the consumption of wine in England, but Gladstone went even further. When, in 1860, he introduced his first measure for lowering the duties on wine, he concurrently brought in a Bill to facilitate its consumption, by granting free scope to keepers of refreshment houses of good character to sell wine on the premises, on payment

of certain Excise licences, irrespective of
magisterial domination. This Bill, which
duly passed into law, was followed by the
" Single Bottle Act " of 1861, which enabled all shopkeepers to retail wine to
be drunk off the premises. Furthermore,
whilst a " dealer " in wine had to pay
ten guineas for a wine-merchant's licence,
" any person (not being a dealer) who
kept a shop for the sale of any goods or
commodities other than foreign wines, in
England and Ireland," was allowed to
sell wine not to be consumed on the premises, by retail, in reputed quart or pint
bottles only, on payment of fifty shillings
for an " off-licence."

This measure proved more far-reaching
than the reduction of duties. It opened
new channels to the activities of grocers,
drapers, limited liability companies promoters, brewers, co-operative societies,
and others. It threw the wine trade open
to all, since every shopkeeper was henceforth free to sell wine on payment of fifty
shillings to the Excise.

Gladstone's wine policy, inaugurated in
1860, has been practically adhered to ever

since; it has, therefore, been given a full fifty years' trial, and we can now form a fair estimate of the influence it has had on the wine trade of England.*

From 1860 till 1876, the clearances of wine from bond show a gradual increase from less than nine million gallons to over eighteen million gallons.

French wines were responsible for the greater share of this remarkable increase. In two single years only, between 1800 and 1860, did the consumption of French wines in England reach half a million gallons; it had even rarely attained 200,000 gallons per annum. In 1860, however, the clearances of French wines from bond amounted to 1,125,599 gallons; in 1862 they were 2,227,662 gallons; and in 1868 they reached 4,502,162 gallons.

But the enormous increase in the clearances from bond of French as well as of other wines, from 1860 till 1876, did not

---

* The present duties on wine are as follows: 1s. 3d. per gallon on wine not exceeding 30 degrees; 3s. per gallon on wine exceeding 30 and not exceeding 42 degrees; still wines imported in bottle are charged an additional duty of 1s. per gallon; sparkling wines are charged an additional duty of 2s·6d. per gallon.

really represent as great an increase in the
actual consumption of wine throughout
the land during that period.

The number of wine sellers had increased
far more rapidly than the number of wine
drinkers. All sorts and conditions of men
entered the wine trade during the twenty
years which followed the reduction of
duties and the passing of the " Single
Bottle Act." All the newcomers had to
build up stocks before they could hope
to do any business ; most of them lacked
the knowledge, and many lacked the means
necessary to embark successfully in the
wine trade. On the other hand, they all
seem to have been possessed of much
energy and of unbounded confidence in
the future. Their energy gained them
some customers, but their enthusiasm led
them to hope for better results than those
they actually obtained, the consequence
being an accumulation of stocks all over
the country.

A few gave up the fight, but others
took up their places, and the consumption not having increased in nearly the
same proportion as either imports or

importers, competition became keener and less fair ; the practice of small profits and cash payments was introduced and rapidly gained ground. It benefited the wine trade at first, by placing wine within the reach of a greater number of people ; this, however, was but a passing benefit, soon to be followed by a serious calamity.

During the seventies, wine was both abundant and excellent, owing to a series of fine vintages, so that remarkable value could be offered to the consumer. Unfortunately, plenty was followed by a woeful scarcity during the eighties, when the phylloxera had devastated the choicest vineyards of France. Good wine became scarce and expensive, and wine-merchants on this side had to ask higher prices. It was then, however, that the " Gladstone " wine-sellers, whose name was legion, committed the fatal mistake of persevering with their low prices and " cheap lines " ; they could only do so by giving very bad quality, but human nature being what we know it to be, the man who allowed himself to be tempted by the low prices offered by ignorant or unscrupulous

dealers, blamed the wine he drank for not
suiting his constitution or his palate, and,
in many cases, he gave up drinking wine
and learnt to resign himself to barley water
and patent medicines.

From 1868 till 1883, the average annual
home consumption of wine was maintained well over 16 million gallons ; then
the check came with the bad vintages,
and from 1884 till 1889 the annual average
was under 14 million gallons. Vineyards
were rapidly replanted, and good wine
was once more made in fair quantity.
Wine-merchants once more replenished
their stocks and the clearances from bond
increased to an annual average of some
15 million gallons from 1890 till 1902.
Whilst stocks of wine and the number
of wine-sellers were again on the increase,
the consumption of wine remained stationary or even decreased. The phylloxera had destroyed vineyards, but low
prices, which spelt bad quality, had destroyed the confidence of a large number
of former wine-drinkers, and this last
evil has been even more disastrous than
the first.

When the real truth of the position became absolutely evident, imports of wine received a serious check; the clearances from bond, from 1903 till 1910 inclusive, gradually decreased and only reached an average of some 12 million gallons per year. In 1911 the clearances of wine from bond were only 11,274,146 gallons, or nearly 7 million less than in 1873, whilst the proportion of wine consumed per head of the population, in 1911, was smaller than the corresponding figure for 1859, when duties were higher and when the wine trade was in the hands of a much smaller number of wine-merchants.

With these figures before us, we cannot but arrive at the conclusion that Gladstone's wine trade policy has failed, not because of the principles on which it rested, but on account of the misuse of the facilities it afforded. Lower duties and a larger number of distributors ought to have widened the field of the wine trade considerably. Unfortunately, too many people sought to avail themselves of the opportunities which were offered;

D

too many, also, whose knowledge of artful and unscrupulous circularising and advertising methods was far greater than their knowledge of wine. A large section of the public has thus had its confidence shaken in the virtues of honest, genuine wine. The consumption of wine in England has consequently gradually decreased, although in nothing like the proportion shown by the official figures of clearances from bond. All over the country existing stocks, the accumulation of many years, have been steadily reduced and have gone into actual consumption.

On the other hand, whilst the consumption of wine in England has been steadily decreasing of late years, lunacy has rapidly increased, and a host of new nervous disorders and diseases of the digestive organs have made their appearance in these, our temperate times.

These facts alone, far more than lengthy arguments and learned treatises on the merits of wine, ought to convince every man whose plain common sense is proof against blind prejudice, that wine is as much a necessity now as it has ever been, all the world over, amongst all peoples, and in all ages.

For verification of this statement, .we have only to turn to the praises bestowed upon wine in the Holy Scriptures and in the works of ancient writers and modern scientists alike ; but no Englishman needs better proofs than those which he will find at almost every page of his country's history.

Saxon kings and Norman lords, churchmen and soldiers, merchants and statesmen, poets and dramatists, all the men who, by their intellect, energy, courage, enterprise, and indomitable spirit on the battlefield, in Parliament, in literature or in commerce, have deserved their country's undying gratitude and the world's admiration or hatred—all were wine drinkers.

From Dunstan, Saxon Edgar's minister, Wolsey, Cromwell, Pitt, down to Disraeli and Gladstone, there has never been a statesman who did not drink wine regularly.

From Chaucer, the son of a royal "Butler," Ben Jonson, Shakespeare, Dryden, Pope, and Addison down to Sir

Walter Scott and Ruskin, the son and grandson of wine-merchants, every poet, dramatist, satirist or novelist has drunk wine and sung its praises.

Wine is, par excellence, the natural food of the brain ; good wine in moderation is one of God's most excellent gifts to man, and whilst it is the duty of the thinking classes to drink wine, it is the duty of the wine-merchant to supply none but good wine.

Wine is like criticism : nothing is more wholesome when good, nothing is more objectionable when bad. Happily, there is quite enough good wine to supply the " élite " who are the wine-drinkers in England, and quite enough good wine-merchants, too, who know their trade and can be trusted. There is no reason to fear, therefore, that the consumption of wine in England will go on decreasing ; it is even safe to assume that it will increase again as soon as wine-drinkers realise that they can get excellent quality and fair value if they will only go to the right man and pay the right price.

He who allows himself to be tempted

by the abnormally low prices of the
wines offered by enterprising circularising experts, deserves no more sympathy
than the sick man who has recourse to
all sorts of widely advertised patent
medicines instead of seeking the advice
of a learned physician.

CHAPTER II

The Vineyards of the World

LONG before the earth had become habitable, before any sign of animal life had appeared either on land or in the seas, the wild Vine grew from pole to pole, in the warm equable temperature which then enveloped the whole globe. At Brjamslak, in Iceland; at Bovey Tracey, in Devonshire; at Sézanne (Marne), in France; in Silesia; in the valley of the Rhine; in Switzerland and in many other parts of Europe as well as in America, fossils have been found, which modern palæontology enables us to recognise as dating back to the earliest stages of the crust formation of the earth, and which show distinct impressions of the leaves of different species of wild vines. Modern science, in this instance, is only confirming the teachings of the book of Genesis, where we read how the vegetable preceded the animal kingdom in the order of creation.

We further learn from Holy Writ how Noah planted a vineyard, and how he drank wine and fell asleep. There is no suggestion, however, that he was the first man who ever drank wine : the fact that he was overcome by it is only incidentally mentioned to bring home the lesson of the undutiful son's conduct and punishment. But, whatever opinions one may have on this point, the fact remains that wine, the naturally fermented juice of the grape, and therefore alcoholic and inebriating when taken in excess, was known, used, and abused, at the earliest known periods of the history of the human race.

Whether it be Osiris, in Egypt ; Varum, in India ; Samschid, in Persia ; Eleusis and Bacchus, in Greece and at Rome ; we find in all the oldest legends of the East and the mythology of the Ancients, a benevolent divinity who was credited with having introduced viticulture and civilisation. It may truly be said that in every part of the world and among every

race, the use of wine is older than the
oldest records which have reached us.

Pickett, in his *Origines Indo-Europé-
ennes*, states that the Aryans introduced
viticulture in Egypt, India, Persia, and
Greece ; this is also the opinion advanced
by Pietro Selleh in his *Trattato di Viti-
coltura e di Vinificazione*.   On the other
hand, we are told by Sir John Malcolm,
in his *History of Persia*, that viticulture
was already flourishing in Persia in the
reign of King Jensheed, a monarch who is
believed to have lived at a very remote
date and who is credited with the dis-
covery of fermentation.   One of his successors, about the year 3000 B.C., is reported
to have undertaken the conquest of the
island of Cyprus, because it contained a
treasure which a mighty king ought to
possess : Wine.

In Egypt, we have more than mere
tradition to rely upon for records of the
greatest antiquity.   Delchevalerie, in his
Illustration Horticole, depicts the scenes
of grape-gathering and wine-making which
ornament the tomb of Phtah-Hotep, who
lived in Memphis some 4000 years before

Christ. Pickering, in his *Chronological History of Plants*, has reproduced similar glyptic illustrations which he ascribes to the Third Egyptian Dynasty, adding that other representations of vineyards and full details of the art of wine-making belong to the Fourth, Seventeenth, and Eighteenth Dynasties. Quite recently, the laws of Khammurabi, King of Babylon about B.C. 2250, have been discovered and decyphered and have aroused a great deal of interest. This sovereign appears to have been the great legislator of his dynasty ; his laws contain the most precise regulations concerning the sale of wine, and show us the poor retailer of wine to have been harassed by a very severe legislation even in those times. Fines were not in vogue then, but the loss of a limb or of life was the penalty incurred by the seller of wine giving bad quality or short measure or allowing riotous conduct on his premises.

In China, viticulture flourished from 2000 B.C. until the fourteenth century of our era, whilst in Europe and in Africa the Phœnicians seem to have taught the

art of wine-making in the Peloponese, the
Latium, Gaul and the Iberic Peninsula,
as well as all along the Mediterranean
coast of Africa where they had colonies.

The earliest records of ancient Greek
and Latin history show that the cultivation of vineyards and the science of wine-
making are coeval with the dawn of civilisation in Greece, the Balkans, Italy,
France, Spain, Portugal, Germany, and
Britain. Modern discoveries of the lake-
dwellings of the Bronze Age, at Castione,
near Parma, at Bex, at Wangen and at
Varese, prove the vine to have been indi-
genous to Europe and that at the remotest
date of western history of which we thus
possess documentary evidence, men grew
corn and vines. Professor Heer, in his
Die Pflanzen der Pfahlbauten, even asserts
that he has been able to distinguish in
some lacustrine remains, evidence of both
wild and cultivated grapes.

The Phœnicians, Greeks and Romans
of old appear to have all realised the
civilising influence of viticulture. Wherever
they obtained a sufficiently secure footing in a new country, they taught

the " Barbarians " to plant and tend vines. At a later date, the same policy was followed by the early Christian missionaries who, wherever they went and whenever they were able to build a church or a monastery as a permanent abode, taught the heathens the gentle art of viticulture. Some of the choicest vineyards of France and Germany retain to this day names recalling their ecclesiastical origin. In Britain, too, it was the early Christian priests who taught the Saxons how to grow vines where no other crop could be raised and, under their guidance, vineyards were planted not only on Kentish chalk and Surrey gravel, but in almost every part of the country, as far north as Scotland.

In more recent times, it was the successors of those early Christian priests who also taught the art of viticulture all along the Pacific coast, from California and Mexico to Peru and Chili.

It is true that the vineyards of Britain, if we except those of the Marquis of Bute, in Wales, and of the Royal Horticultural Society, in Surrey, have long ceased to exist, as well as those of Normandy, Belgium, and Northern Germany. This is not, however, because vines can no longer be grown in northern latitudes, but because it has been found more profitable for centuries past to obtain supplies from those foreign lands where the climate, soil and cheaper labour, make it possible to produce wine of better quality and at lower cost.

The vine will grow in all but arctic and tropical latitudes, but its fruit will only mature to perfection in temperate countries.

To give an account of every vineyard at present existing in the world is a task far too difficult to attempt here and one which would greatly exceed the limits of this volume. Let us be content, therefore, with a few general remarks concerning the more important and more interesting vineyards of the world, particularly those which produce the wines most popular in England.

FRANCE

Of all wine producing countries, France is unequalled not only for the quantity,

but also for the quality and the great
variety of wines she produces.

The country is divided into eighty-
six " Départements " of which all, with
the exception of the eight most northern,
produce wine. The yearly average production of wine in France is over 1,300
million gallons of wine. By way of
a comparison, it may be remarked that
the average yearly consumption of French
wines in the United Kingdom is only
about 3½ million gallons, and that whilst
the consumption of wine in France is
26 gallons per head of the population,
it is only a quarter of one gallon in England. It is also worthy of notice that,
whilst the consumption of wine is 100
times greater in France than in England
per head of the population, drunkenness
is very seldom met with on the other
side of the Channel and alcoholism is
very much less prevalent amongst our
neighbours than in our own country.
This is all the more remarkable when one
considers that France has never had the
benefit of that large number of enthusiastic
and energetic total abstinence societies

which have flourished in our midst so
long and expended so much money and
labour to combat drunkenness.

The vineyards of France which interest us most in England are those which
produce Sparkling Champagne and Saumur, Cognac Brandy, Burgundies and
Claret.

BORDEAUX

Ever since the fourth century, when
Ausonius, who was born at Bordeaux
in A.D. 309, tells us that they were in
demand in Rome, the wines of Bordeaux
have been shipped to every part of the
civilised world and have enjoyed a more
universal and lasting reputation than any
other wine. But not all the wines which
have for so many centuries passed
through Bordeaux on their way to distant
and less-favoured lands, have been the
produce of the Bordeaux vineyards. What
we call Claret, in England, and what
the French call Vin de Bordeaux is, or
should be, the produce of the " Département " of the Gironde, and of no other.
In all the neighbouring " Départements,"

vineyards have existed for centuries past and still flourish ; the wines they produce, however, are not entitled to the name of Bordeaux because they are shipped from that port. They were known in England in mediæval times as red, white, or claret wines from Guienne, Gascony or Languedoc. The appellation " Claret " was at first used to designate the style and not the origin of the wine, but as practically the whole of the light red wines consumed in England came primarily from Bordeaux, the meaning of the name Claret became gradually restricted first to those red and white wines shipped from Bordeaux and later to the Bordeaux wines proper, or the produce of the Gironde. Custom having endowed the name of Claret with a strictly limited geographical meaning, it should not be used in conjunction with any other geographical appellation ; it is as illogical to speak of California Claret, for instance, as of Tarragona Port or Italian Champagne.

The Département of the Gironde is part of the old Province of Guienne and produces a much greater quantity of fine red and white wines than any other Département.

The vineyards of the Gironde may be divided into six principal districts, namely : (1) Médoc ;   (2) Graves ;   (3) Sauternes ; (4) Entre-deux-Mers ; (5) Côtes ; and (6) Palus.   All these districts are situated on the Garonne, on the Dordogne, or on their confluent, the Gironde, and produce an average of 91,895,019 gallons per annum.

ħ The MEDOC is a strip of low lying land along the left bank of the River Gironde, some six miles wide and about 50 miles long. The best vineyards are planted on a series of gently swelling elevations of varying heights, which may be likened to some great downs, the soil of which is chiefly composed of silicious gravel and is sometimes of a calcareous nature.

The principal vineyards of the Médoc, as one leaves Bordeaux and proceeds towards the Bay of Biscay, lie in the districts of Ludon, Macau and Labarde, and on to Cantenac and Margaux, from the stony and gravelly soil of which are produced some of the most delicate and refined of all clarets.

After passing through some few miles of flat country where richer alluvial soil is to be met and a somewhat poorer quality of wine is made, one comes to the vineyards of St. Laurent, and the more famous district of St. Julien, in which Léoville, Larose and many other fine growths are situated. From there, one passes into the Pauillac district, where are to be found some of the finest vineyards in all the Médoc. Here, near the old-fashioned village of Pauillac, on the banks of the broad river, are the celebrated Châteaux of Lafite and Latour, Mouton, Pichon Longueville and Pontet Canet, and more than a score of others, separated from each other and from less famous vineyards merely by a road or even a path.

After leaving Château Lafite, one enters the St. Estèphe district where there are fewer Châteaux, but where some very fine wine is also made. At St. Estèphe may be said to terminate the "Grands Crûs du Médoc," although there is a large quantity of good wine made in districts beyond.

2. GRAVES.—-This district is smaller but more picturesque than the Médoc, beginning just outside Bordeaux and extending only thirteen miles to the south, and about five and a half miles to the west of the city. The soil is of a light sandy nature full of silicious stones of different sizes and colour to a depth of from two to ten feet. The subsoil varies a good deal, and is either clay, chalk or stone, or formed of a hard kind of very dark sand, known as alios, which contains a ferrugineous matter called " arène." There, again, we have a soil absolutely unfit for any other culture but that of the vine, which grows there and produces a wine the flavour and sweetness of which more than compensate for the usually small quantity of the yield. The Graves district produces red as well as white wines of very high repute, but the brightest jewel in its vinous crown, and one of which it is justly proud, is the Château Haut Brion, which stands at the very gates of Bordeaux.

3. SAUTERNES.—This is a comparatively small   district,   comprising   Sauternes,

Bommes and Barsac, and dedicated almost entirely to white wines. The soil differs from that of the Graves district, which it adjoins; it is a mixture of clay and gravel partly, and clay and chalk.

The sunny vineyards of the Sauternes district produce a naturally sweet wine, of unsurpassed excellence, the best and most widely known being that of Château Yquem.

4. ENTRE-DEUX-MERS.—This district is situated ·between the Garonne and the Dordogne and produces a great deal of sound and useful red and white wines.

5. CÔTES.—The *Côtes* wines are those grown on the hills in several parts of the Gironde Département, and vary therefore greatly in quantity and quality. By far the finest Côtes wines are those of the St. Emilion district on the right bank of the Dordogne. This is quite the most attractive district of the Gironde as it is undulating and abounds in beautiful landscape whilst the old ruins of St. Emilion itself are of great beauty and archæological interest.

6. PALUS.—The Palus wines are those

obtained from vineyards planted in rich
alluvial soil either close to the banks of
the Gironde, the Garonne, or the Dordogne,
on islands in these rivers or in the plains.
These vineyards give usually abundant
crops but the quality of the wine made
therefrom is distinctly inferior to the produce of any of the other vineyards of the
Gironde.

COGNAC

Cognac is the name of a small town on
the river Charente, in the heart of a wine-
growing district which produces the finest
brandies in the world. As far back as
the reign of King John, and for many centuries afterwards, the wines of Saintonge,
Aunis and Angoumois were shipped to
England as Rochelle wines and sold at
cheaper rates than any other. These wines
were considered thin and light then and
such are still their characteristics to-day;
but, if the wines from the Charentes
vineyards have never been very fine, they
yield, when distilled, a brandy of excep-
tional excellence and inimitable character.

The only brandy entitled to the name
Cognac is that which has been distilled

from wine produced by the vines grown in a limited district, the *Région Délimitée;* this comprises the greater part of the two Départements of Charente and Charente Inférieure, and a small area in the two other neighbouring Départements of Deux Sèvres, in the north, and Dordogne, in the south.

The vineyards of the Cognac producing district may be divided in two main classes, the *Champagnes* and the *Bois.*

On the left bank of the river Charente, and in the western part of the Département of Charente, are situated the vineyards of the *Grande Champagne* and *Petite Champagne,* which produce the finest brandies. On the opposite side of the river Charente, there is a small district known as *Borderies,* where brandy of excellent quality is also made.

The soil of the *Grande* and *Petite Champagnes* is chiefly calcareous ; in the *Borderies,* the soil is of a similar nature, but the chalk it consists of is of a harder kind than in the *Champagnes.* From the vineyards of these three districts is produced a distinctive and constant type of brandy of

greater finesse and excellence than any
other, and one which no connoisseur can
fail to identify.

Outside these principal growths, however, the quality, flavour and distinctive
properties of the brandies made in the rest
and greater part of the *Région Délimitée*,
vary to a very considerable extent,
according to the nature of the soil and
the climatic conditions of each particular
locality. There are a very large number
of *Bois* of various grades and types, which
are known as *Fins Bois*, *Bons Bois*, *Bois
Ordinaires* and *Bois Eloignés*.

The vines grown on clayish soil in the
eastern part of the *Région*, and those from
more western vineyards, close to the Atlantic, where the soil is very sandy and
the climate damp, produce two very
different types of brandies, both, however,
belonging to the same class of *Bois
Eloignés*.

In other words, whilst *Grande Champagne*, *Petite Champagne* and *Borderies*
are geographical expressions corresponding to the peculiar chalky soil formation
of a distinctly limited area, the different

Bois are geographical appellations corresponding to the quality of brandies made
in specified parts of the Région Délimitée,
whatever differences may exist between
the soil, the climate, the aspect and the
finished product of each particular growth or
" terroir."

BURGUNDY

The ancient province of Burgundy is
represented chiefly by the Départements
of the Côte d'Or, the Sâone et Loire and
the Yonne. Of these, the first produces
the finest wines and owes its name to a
series of hills, about 36 miles in length,
which stretch from Dijon to Chalon-sur-
Sâone in the direction of the N.N.E. to
S.S.W., the aspect of their vine-clad slopes
being principally towards the east, south
east and also south. These hills have a
height of from 200 to 300 feet and consist
chiefly of a very hard kind of calcareous
soil whilst the subsoil is marl and rock.

The vineyards of the Côte d'Or begin
generally on the upper third of the hills,
never ascending to the brow, and they
stretch down the incline towards the plain,
and sometimes extend for a mile or two

in the plain itself. The best vineyards
are never in the plain nor on the upper
part of the slopes but on the middle or the
lower part of the inclines which are nowhere very steep. From Dijon in the
north, to Santenay in the south, are to be
found the finest Burgundy vineyards, all
of which are in the Département of the
Côte d'Or. Some five miles from Dijon is
Gevrey, where Chambertin is grown ; then
one passes Musigny and the world-famous
Clos-Vougeot, where the soil is quite different from that of adjoining vineyards,
being a mixture of lime on a subsoil of
clay. Further on is Vosnes, where are
to be found the vineyards of Romanée
St. Vivant, Romanée Conti, La Tache
and Richebourg, all of which produce
most excellent wines. After Vosnes, one
comes to Nuits, where the ground faces
south-west and is almost flat, and then to
Beaune, after passing Aloxe, chiefly famous
for the produce of the Corton vineyards.
After Beaune, where the old hospice may
be said to reign over the vine-land of
Burgundy, one comes to Volnay, Pom-
mard, Meursault, and then to the most

famous white wine vineyards of the Côte
d'Or at Montrachet. Chassagne, not far
from Puligny, and Santenay, on the border
of the Côte d'Or, also possess many good
vineyards. In the adjoining Départment
of Sâone et Loire, many fair vineyards
are also to be seen and much good wine
is made there, but none which can compare in quality with the best growths of
the Côte d'Or. The best red wines of
Sâone et Loire are those of Mâcon and the
best white ones those of Pouilly.

In quite another direction, the Département of the Yonne, part of which used to
be within the limits of the old province of
Burgundy, produces a very large quantity
of red and white wines of which the white
wines of Chablis are the most celebrated.

South of the Département of Sâone et
Loire is that of the Rhône, where are the
Beaujolais hills which produce an agreeable wine, lighter but also much cheaper
than the Côte d'Or wines.

Further south, and still on the left
bank of the Rhône, at Tain, are the vineyards which produce the red and white
wines of Hermitage.

In the whole of the valley of the Rhône, as well as in the whole of the south of France, from the Alps to the Pyrenees, vineyards are to be seen and wine is made, but we must return northwards to other vineyards which produce a wine more popular than any other in our country : Champagne.

CHAMPAGNE

Champagne is the name of an ancient French province, where the Romans introduced viticulture and where it has flourished ever since. It is also the name of a sparkling white wine known by that name all the world over ; but, although the old province of Champagne was divided in 1789 into four Départements, the Ardennes, Aube, Marne and Haute Marne, all of which boast that they possess extensive vineyards and produce good wine, the better class Champagne is grown within a comparatively small area of the Marne Département only.

The grapes which produce the best Sparkling Champagne are grown on the calcareous slopes of two distinct ranges of hills, with greatly varying aspects, north, east and south, but all possessing one common and important feature, namely, poor soil, practically all chalk, and unsuitable for any other culture.

The Champagne vineyards are usually classed into two main topographical divisions, those of the *Rivière* and those of the *Montagne de Reims*. The former are facing the River Marne and may be further divided as follows :—(1) The vineyards of the River proper, facing south, from Cumières to Avenay, and including besides these, Hautvillers, Dizy, Mareuil-sur-Ay, and Ay ; (2) The Epernay vineyards, which also include the neighbouring growths of Pierry and Chouilly ; (3) The Montagne d'Avize, a gentle range of hills beginning with Grauves and Cuis in the west and sloping towards the east as far as Vertus. From Cuis to Vertus are the finest Champagne white-grape vineyards, at Cramant, Avize, Le Mesnil and Oger. Owing to their north-easterly aspect, most of these vineyards are liable to be severely affected by late spring frosts, which are responsible for the smaller average yield per acre in that district than in any of the others of the same region.

What is known as the Montagne de Reims is really the other side of the range of hills which face the river Marne and divide Reims from Epernay. On the Reims side, the slopes are not nearly so steep and permit of a far greater acreage of hillside vineyards, beginning at Ville-domange. To the east of this, and practically facing north, are the famous vine-yards of Rilly-la-Montagne, Chigny, Ludes, Mailly, Verzenay, Sillery and Verzy. Soon after Verzy, the *Montagne* comes to an end in the shape of an irregular horse-shoe or spur, and round the bend with a southern aspect are the vineyards of Bouzy, Ambonnay and Trépail.

All the above are first growths and produce none but the best Champagne. There are, of course, a great many other less renowned vineyards within the Marne Département alone, and within the area officially delimited by the French Govern-ment, outside which no wine can be made which is to be sold as Cham-pagne.

SAUMUR

The Département of Maine et Loire, where Saumur is situated, produces a large quantity of wine, chiefly white and still, which possesses great delicacy. In mediæval times, the still white wines of Anjou were largely shipped from Nantes to England, and were greatly appreciated. We only know now, in this country, the sparkling wines made on the low calcareous hills in the neighbourhood of Saumur.

GERMANY

Antiquarian finds of Roman wine cups and wine-making implements in Germany, as well as the writings of ancient Roman historians, can leave no doubt whatsoever as to the antiquity of viticulture in Germany. It is not so generally known, however, that the trade in Rhine and Moselle wines was flourishing in England as far back as the reigns of Edgar, Ethelred II., and Edward the Confessor.

Viticulture, in Germany, and the imports of German wines into this country have never attained and never can attain a very

considerable development. Vines will only
grow within a comparatively small area of
the German Empire, but they still flourish
where they have been growing for many
centuries past, lovingly tended by a hard-
working race of vine-growers, who are
assisted and encouraged by intelligent and
strictly enforced laws. On the other hand,
the trade in German wines in this country
still holds the very honourable place which
it has enjoyed for so many centuries.

The average imports of German wines in
the United Kingdom are about 600,000
gallons per annum, whilst the average total
production of wine in Germany is only about
fifty-four million gallons per year. We,
therefore, consume over one per cent. of
the wines of Germany, whilst we only receive 0·28 per cent. of the wines of France,
and 0·02 of those of Italy.*

The following Table shows the number of
acres planted with vines in 1909 and the
number of gallons of wine they yielded per
year, taking the average of the years 1907,
1908, and 1909.

---

* We receive about 0·74 per cent. of the wine-production
of Spain and 3·45 per cent. of that of Portugal.

	Acres.				Gallons.
Alsace Lorraine	73,246	yielding an average of	15,980,002
Bavaria -	52,903	,,	,,	,,	11,924,336
Prussia -	43,472	,,	,,	,,	7,284,766
Baden -	41,276	,,	,,	,;	8,594,978
Wurtemburg	39,143	,,	,,	,,	4,939,284
Hesse -	32,823	,,	,,	,,	5,274,957
Other Districts	491	,.	,,	,,	93,629
Total -	283,354				54,091,952

or an average production per acre of :—

640	gallons in	Alsace Lorraine.
552	,,	Bavaria.
255	,,	Prussia.
543	,,	Baden.
281	,,	Wurtemburg.
297	,,	Hesse.
477	,,	other districts.

Practically the whole of the German vineyards are in southern and western provinces of the Empire, and the German wines shipped to this country come chiefly from three distinct districts, viz., (1) From the valleys of the Moselle and its tributaries ; (2) from the valley of the Rhine ; (3) from the Bavarian Palatinate.

MOSELLE

The wines generally known in this country as Moselle wines, are the produce of the finest growths of the valley of the Moselle from Treves to Coblenz, as well as of the vineyards which grace the banks of the Saar and of the Ruwer, two tributaries of the Moselle.

The valley of the Upper Moselle, before the river reaches Treves, produces a large quantity of wine, but none of superior quality, and none which can compare with the wines of the Saar. This river runs mostly in a north-westerly direction, and joins the Moselle a few miles above Treves. The finest vineyards of the Saar are on the right bank of the river from Geisberg in the south, to Euchariusberg in the north. Not far from Geisberg is Bockstein, and a little further on the famous Scharzhofberg, the finest growth of the Saar valley. Two other celebrated Bergs in the district are Scharzberg and Agritiusberg, whilst excellent wines are also made a little further north at Wiltingen and Oberemmel.

Below the ancient city of Treves, rich in Roman remains of great beauty, the Moselle receives, on the right, another small river, called the Ruwer. In the valley of the Ruwer, some very delicate and fascinating wines are also made, none better known nor more excellent than those from the ancient ecclesiastical vineyards at Grünehaus.

From there to Coblenz, on either bank of the Moselle, are grown the finest wines of the Moselle proper. To name but a few : there are Piesport and the range of the Brauneberg hills, on the left bank of the river ; a little further down, and on the opposite bank, we come to the celebrated Berncastel vineyards, where the vines grow on distinctly slaty soil.

From Berncastel northwards, the vineyards of Graach, Josephshof, Wehlen, Zeltingen and Trarbach, on the right, and those of Erden, Machern and Uerzig, on the left, are among those which produce the most delicate Moselle wines, light without being thin, and possessing that very distinctive bouquet which is their greatest charm. The peculiar aroma of the Moselle wines is due to the silicious soil on which they are grown, which is more or less hard

F

according to each district, but which often requires blasting before the vines can be planted.

The lower valley of the Moselle offers one of the most picturesque and delightful sights it is possible to see. Nowhere in the world can more perfectly ideal scenery be found than in the Moselle valley on a fine summer day. The winding river sparkling in the sun ; the steep vine-clad hills crowned with secular oaks ; the quaint little villages nestling among vineyards by the riverside ; the gable roofs of old houses closely grouped round some sturdy grey church ; the grim tower of some ancient castle standing above it all on some inaccessible rock ; there is no vine-land which possesses greater beauty or greater charm.

THE RHINE

The valley of the Rhine is not so picturesque as that of the Moselle, but it has more grandeur. From Bonn to Coblenz and from Coblenz to Bingen many vineyards are to be seen on either bank of the river, and much wine is made, most of which, however, is consumed in Germany. Abroad,

the most celebrated Rhine wines are those
of a limited district known as the Rheingau
and those of Rhenish Hessen.

The Rheingau vineyards proper are on
the right bank of the Rhine and may be
said to begin opposite Bingen, with the
extensive vineyards of Rudesheim, and to
end with the hills of Rauenthal. It is
within that comparatively small area that
are to be found the most famous Rheingau
vineyards which yield wines second to
none in the world in point of excellence and
which are eagerly bought, at the vintage,
at prices far higher than those given
for new wines in any other vine-growing
country.

After leaving Rudesheim, one comes to
Geisenheim, Winkel, Mittelheim and Oes-
trich, near the Rhine, whilst higher up the
hills are the Castles of Johannisberg and
Voirads surrounded by magnificent vineyards. A little further east are the no less
celebrated hills of Steinberg, whilst nearer
the river are the famous growths of Hatten-
heim, Marcobrunnen, Erbach and Eltville.

On the opposite bank of the Rhine, in
Hessen, there are a far greater number of

vineyards from Bingen to Mayence and
from Mayence to Worms, than in the
Rheingau, but there is only a comparatively small percentage of the wines made
in this province which can claim to possess a
very high degree of excellence.   Some vineyards in Hessen, however, produce very
fine wines, with good body and bouquet,
which are eminently suited for exporta-
tion.   The best of these are the wines of
Nierstein and Oppenheim, some miles south
of Mayence, and those of Liebfraumilch,
near Worms, on the southern frontier of
Hessen.

As regards the tributaries of the Rhine
other than the Moselle, the Ahr and the
Nahe, on the left, the Lahn, the Main and
the Neckar, on the right, are the most
important ones.   Extensive vineyards are
cultivated in the valleys of all these rivers,
and they produce both red and white wines
in large quantity and of very good quality.
Walporzheim, on the Ahr, and Hockheim,
on the Main, are the two most celebrated
growths of these tributaries of the Rhine,
the first being famous for its red wines, and
the second for its white wines.   It is said

that Hock, the name so generally given in
England to all Rhine wines, and sometimes
to all German wines, is derived from Hockheim, the wines of which have been justly
popular among us for many centuries.

PALATINATE

The Palatinate Vineyards differ from all
others in Germany, being the only ones
which are not grown in sheltered valleys,
on the steep slopes of the hills which border
the Rhine and its tributaries. They are
situated on a plateau, protected from
strong winds by a mountain range, and are
planted in a soil chiefly of alluvial origin,
mostly with southern aspects. The wines
made in that district are very distinct
from those of the Rheingau, being more
luscious but not always so lasting. The
first growths of the *Palatinate* are Deides-
heim and Forst ; also Durkheim, Wachen-
heim, and Ruppertsberg.

PORTUGAL

Portugal, as well from its geographical
position, benignant climate and geological conformation, as from other propitious

circumstances, is admirably adapted to
viticulture. Vines are grown and wines
are made in many parts of Portugal, but
the only wines which will bear exporting
are those grown in the immediate vicinity
of Lisbon and in the valley of the Douro.
Some 200 years ago the wines of Lisbon
were more prized in London than those of
Oporto, whilst we received up to the middle
of the last century a fairly large quantity
of white Lisbon wines, Collares, Bucellas
and Carcavellos from Portugal. Our trade
in wines with Portugal is, however, now
confined almost entirely to those shipped
from Oporto, and the vineyards which
produce Port are really the only ones which
need arrest our attention.

Port is the produce of certain vineyards
situated on the banks of the River Douro,
within a strictly limited area. The name
Port, therefore, has a well-defined geographical meaning, and does not only
indicate the style or quality of a wine, but
also and chiefly the country and district
of origin of that wine. There is some red
wine made in Spain, in Cape Colony,
Australia and California, which may have

the same colour and the same alcoholic
strength as Port, but no such wine should
rightly be sold as Port, even with the
adjunct of the locality it really comes from.

The hills of the Douro valley are very
high and often very steep, but they are
covered from base to summit with vines,
chiefly planted in tiers and terraces which
it has only been possible to make by cutting or blasting the hard mountain rock.
Vines grown in the valleys produce less
fine wine than those planted higher up
the hills, although the latter, if too high
up, run the risk of being scorched, the
sun beating with merciless severity on the
rock.

SPAIN

Spain possesses a temperate climate and
a generally arid calcareous soil highly con-
genial to the culture of the vine. From
north to south and from east to west,
sites, soils and aspects of the happiest
kind are to be met with in every part of
the country, and luxuriant vineyards are to
be seen on the slopes of almost every hill
or mountain ; yet there is but a small
percentage of the vinous wealth of Spain

ever sent abroad, and the only Spanish
wines of any commercial importance in
our country, are those of Jerez and
Malaga in the south and those of Tarragona in the north.

The fame of the Jerez wines in England
is of great antiquity and was even greater
than that of any other wine during the
latter part of the sixteenth century. By
an order of March 14th, 1517, renewed
in 1530, the Duke of Medina Sidonia
granted special privileges to all Englishmen who went to Seville, Cadiz or Jerez
to buy wines. The wine called Sack which
is so often praised in Shakespeare's plays
and the works of all the old poets and
dramatists, was Spanish wine which chiefly
came from Port St. Mary.

The same vineyards which produced
the Sack of old now yield sherry. Car-
bonate of lime forms about two-thirds of
the soil, and the sun ripens the grapes
without those hazards from frosts or excessive rains to which in more northern
climes the vintage is constantly liable.

To the east of Jerez, on the other side
of the Sierras are the vineyards of Malaga,

by far the most picturesque in Spain. The mountains round Malaga are clothed from the valley depths to the summits with vines, and the low-roofed houses of the peasants clinging to the mountain side look as if they had been placed by an artist's hand. Many of the vineyards are located at a great height from the level of the sea and planted on narrow terraces.

Tarragona, in Catalonia, produces a very large quantity of wines, chiefly red, which are largely exported to this country, where they are of great value principally for blending purposes.

ITALY

Italy is, after France, the largest wine-producing country of the world, and it may be said to be one large vineyard from Lombardy and Tuscany in the north, down to Sicily in the extreme south.

Some sparkling wines are made on the low hills of the Asti and Montferrat region, whilst dry red wines are made in very large quantities in Tuscany. These are both pleasant and wholesome, although

they are exported to this country only
in comparatively small quantities. The
most renowned white Italian wines are
those from the vineyards of Capri, whilst
Marsala produces a large quantity of
luscious wines of great excellence.

OTHER COUNTRIES

SWITZERLAND, AUSTRIA-HUNGARY, the
BALKAN STATES, GREECE and TURKEY,
all boast more or less extensive vineyards and produce a considerable quantity
of wines, some of which are of rare excellence, such as the renowned imperial
Tokay from Hungary. In the Crimea,
the Caucasus and Bessarabia, there are
no less than 650,700 acres of vineyards
which produce an average of 77,336,000
gallons of wine per year.

AFRICA also possesses vast vineyards,
chiefly in Algeria and Tunis in the north,
and in Cape Colony in the south.

AMERICA possesses many vineyards.
The vine grows and wine is made in
Canada and in many parts of the United
States, but nowhere in such quantities
nor to such perfection as in California.

Mexico, Peru, Bolivia and Chili all produce a certain quantity of wine which is mostly consumed locally or in neighbouring States. On the other side of the Andes, in the Argentine Republic, the vineyards of Mendoza are the most important. Uruguay and Brazil also have extensive vineyards, but none of these South American Republics have begun exporting their wines to the Old World.

Not so, however, AUSTRALIA, in whose vineyards on an average 4½ million gallons of wine are produced per year, a large proportion of which is annually exported to England.

CYPRUS, the Azores, the Canary islands and Madeira are the principal vineyard islands which produce excellent wines, some of which are sent to this country every year.

This rapid survey of the vineyards of the world teaches us that the vine is not only one of the most ancient of the plants we know, but that it is also one of the most universal. It holds a unique place in the marvellously ordained economy

of our wonderful world, being at the
same time the most fruitful of all plants
or trees and the only one which will
grow—and is meant by nature to grow
—in the most barren soils. This is so
true, that it may be safely asserted that
the poorer the soil the better will be
the wine. A poor light chalky soil such
as at Cognac, Avize or Jerez ; sandy,
stony gravel, as in Médoc ; decomposed
granite as at Hermitage ; soft or hard
slate as on the banks of the Moselle ;
hard schist or granite as in the valley
of the Douro; soils which are not suitable for either corn, beet nor even grass,
there will the vine grow and prosper.

On the other hand, and as a consequence
of the poor soil of most vineyards, it
may be asserted that no other culture
requires so much individual intelligence
and incessant care as does viticulture.
So that the vine does not only hold a
prominent position economically, rendering valuable otherwise valueless lands,
but also and chiefly socially, as a civilising agent. The vine is *par excellence* the
plant of peaceful lands ; nomadic Arabs

and roaming Gipsies sow corn and root crops but move on as soon as their harvest is gathered. Not so the vine-grower, whose patient and arduous labours can never be repaid until some years after he has planted those vines which attach him to the soil and which he learns to tend with that loving and intelligent care the like of which is not to be found in any other branch of agriculture.

AVERAGE OFFICIAL PRODUCTION OF WINE
PER ANNUM (1907–1908–1909).

Countries.	Gallons.
France - - - - -	1,333,728,022
Italy - - - - -	1,078,362,032
Spain - - - -	378,935,084
Algeria - - - -	180,646,994
Austria - - - -	136,730,792
Portugal - - - -	84,333,326
Hungary - - - -	77,183,326
Russia - - - - -	57,200,000
Germany - - - -	56,088,758
Chili - - - -	49,866,652
Roumania - - - -	47,666,652
Greece - - - -	45,650,000
Bulgaria - - - -	45,466,652
United States of America -	35,933,326
Turkey and Cyprus -	35,200,000
Argentine Republic -	26,766,652
Switzerland - - -	22,806,520
Servia - - - -	12,320,000
Brazil - - - -	8,286,652
Tunis - - - -	6,233,326
Australia - - -	4,490,200
Cape Colony - - -	4,228,400
Azores, Canaries, Madeira -	2,933,326
Luxemburg - - -	2,449,326
Peru - - - -	2,192,652
Uruguay - - - -	2,170,652
Bolivia - - - -	638,000
Persia - - - -	337,326
Mexico - - - -	293,326
	3,739,237,974

CHAPTER III

The Vine and its Fruit

WINE is as old as the oldest records we possess of the world's history, and the vine, one of God's noblest gifts to man, is more ancient, more universal as well as more fruitful than any other plant or tree we know.

Although wine is but the fermented juice of the grape, it is better adapted to the particular constitution, peculiar temperament and personal tastes of individual men and women than any other of bountiful Nature's products.

The vineyards of the world have produced for many centuries past—and still produce—such a variety of wines, such a diversity of types and styles, that rich and poor, in health and in sickness, during the parching heat of the summer and the bitter cold of the winter, we have at our command wines either cheap or dear, cooling or comforting, sweet or dry, still or sparkling, and always grateful to the palate as well as refreshing to body and mind alike.

The great variety of the different sorts of wines we know is due chiefly to two causes of paramount importance :

Firstly, to the type, nature and state of the grapes from which the must or grape juice is obtained.

Secondly, to the different methods of vinification used in transforming the must or grape juice into wine.

The grape is the fruit of the vine, and the juice of the ripe grape is more or less acid or luscious, and contains different characteristics which will assert themselves after fermentation, according to three principal factors.

Firstly, the species of the vine.

Secondly, the nature of the soil on which the vine was grown.

Thirdly, the climate of the district where it was grown and of the year when it was grown.

SPECIES

The vine holds an important place of its own in botany. It belongs to the great family of the *Ampelidacæ* (from the Greek, *Ampelos*, vine), but the genus *Vitis* is the only one which needs arrest our attention.

The genus *Vitis* includes all grape-bearing vines ; there are ten different groups of Asiatic *Vitis*, sixteen American ones, and one European, the *Vitis Vinifera*.

Until the last century, there was practically no other vine but the *Vitis Vinifera* in Europe, where it had been cultivated without interruption ever since the days of the Phœnicians. As a result of so many centuries of observation of and experiments with the *Vitis Vinifera*, the European parent vine possesses a far greater number of different varieties than any other species. It also produces grapes of a better quality than any other class of vine, either Asiatic or American, but, on the other hand, it is far less fruitful and usually less hardy than these. One may form some

G

idea of the considerable variety of European *Vitis Vinifera* types from the fact that, in 1844, when a catalogue was published of the different sorts of vines then being reared in the Luxembourg Gardens, in Paris, there were over 2,000 names of distinct types of *Vitis Vinifera*, all of which had been obtained from the vine-growing districts of France alone.

A long list of the endless varieties of *Vitis Vinifera* would serve no useful purpose, and we shall only name a few of the principal types of grapes which produce the finest wines and brandies in the world.

In the Médoc, the best red wines are obtained from the Cabernet, Malbec and Merlot vines.

In the Sauternais, the finest white wines are the produce of the Semillon, Sauvignon and Muscadelle vines.

In the Charentes, the Folle Blanche produces the finest brandies.

In Burgundy, Pinots produce the best wines. but the Gamays, in the plains, give the greater quantity of wine.

In the Beaujolais, the Gamay vine is the most extensively cultivated.

At Hermitage, the Petite Syrah vine is responsible for the finest red wines.

In the Marne, Pinots produce the best Champagne wines.

At Saumur, the Chenin Blanc is the vine chiefly cultivated for white wines.

In Germany, the Riesling grape produces the finest wines. The Traminer grape is cultivated on a smaller scale, but also for fine wines. The Sylvaner and different varieties of the Burgundy Pinots are also extensively grown.

In the Douro Valley, the Bastardo, Touriga, Alvarelhao, Gouveio, Tinta Cao, Tinta Francisca, and other vines are cultivated simultaneously.

In Spain, the Pedro Jimenes, the Palomino, the Moscatel, the Monterey and the Montuopile vines produce the finest wines.

In Italy, the Nebbiolo, Barbera and Nocera produce the best red wines, and the Trebbiano the best white wines.

In Austria, the Burgundy Pinots and German Rieslings are extensively grown.

but there are also many local varieties
of vines.

In Hungary, the Furmint vine produces the famous Tokay wine.

In Russia, they grow in the South
over sixty different species of Russian
vines.

In North America, the *Vitis Vinifera*
has been introduced, but the vines
mostly grown there, both in the Eastern
States and along the Pacific Coast,
where the most extensive vineyards are
situated, are the numerous hybrids of
the different American vines, chiefly those
of the Rupestres, Ripariæ, and Labruscæ
species. The Catawba vines, the praises
of which were sung by Longfellow, belong
to the last-named group.

In the vineyards of South America,
many varieties of the European *Vitis
Vinifera* have been acclimatised and are
being grown with success.

In Australia, many of the best
European species of the *Vitis Vinifera*
were introduced as far back as 1830, most
of which it has been found possible to
grow well.

SOIL

The species of the vine affects the style and quality of the wine, but the nature of the soil affects the growth and the produce of different species of vines in a very remarkable way. If cultivated with proper care, pippins and codlins will grow equally well in England, France, Germany, America and Australia, and will produce the same kind of fruit everywhere, although the abundance of the crop may vary ; but no King Pippin will ever yield a crop of baking apples, nor will a Keswick Codlin ever produce crab apples, whatever the soil or the climate of the district they may be grown in.

It is quite different with the vine. The large family of Pinots, for instance, give excellent results in Burgundy, Champagne, Germany and Austria, but the grapes they yield in these different countries and the wines made therefrom vary so much, that one can hardly realise that they are produced by the same species of vine. In each case, the nature of the soil has altered the

characteristics of the species very considerably. In this instance, the same
species of vine, finding suitable soil and
environments under different conditions,
adapts itself to its near circumstances and
produces wines of the same degree of
excellence although very different in all
other respects.

In many other vine-growing districts
of Europe, America, Africa, and Australia
the Pinots cannot be acclimatised
at all, whilst in other parts they grow
but give disappointing results. In the
Beaujolais, for instance, which is very
close to the Côte d'Or, the Pinots produce a wine distinctly inferior to that
made from the Gamay vines, which belong
to a commoner species, but are better suited
to the soil and climate of the Beaujolais.
In the South of France, the Pinots not
only can grow but even grow with such
vigour in a soil too rich for them, that
they yield an abundance of grapes from
which no good wine can be made.

On the other hand, the Gamay vines
which give very good results in the Beaujolais, and the Aramon vines which are

grown with great success in the South of France, never could produce any good wine if planted at Clos de Vougeot, Ay or Rudesheim. In other words, the nature of the soil has such an effect upon the species of the vine, that fine wines can only be made when the right species of vines are grown in exactly the right kind of soil.

The Médoc Cabernet vines will not produce a Château Margaux at the Cape, any more than the Folle Blanche of the Charentes can produce Cognac brandy in the Languedoc or the Burgundy Pinots Chambertin in Austria, the German Rieslings Johannisberg wine in California or the Palomino grape Sherry in Chili.

There can be no perfection without harmony, [and perfect harmony between species and soil is absolutely indispensable to the production of fine wines.

ASPECT

Besides the different species of vines and the nature of the soil in which they are grown, the quality of a wine depends also on the climate, altitude, and aspect of the vineyards.

The vine requires a certain amount of heat and moisture as well as a good deal of air and solar light. This is the reason why practically all the best wines are grown on hills or inclines often so steep as to necessitate tiers or terraces which allow the sun to bathe each vine and let the air circulate freely.

In Germany and the more northern vineyards of France, the cultivation of vines on inclines also secures for them a greater amount of heat and a better safeguard against the risks of spring frosts. In the south of France, where the heat is quite sufficient to mature grapes completely when grown in the plains, the quality of the wines made from hill-side vineyards or Côtes is superior to the wines from the plain. In the Cognac, Médoc and Graves districts, the proximity of the Atlantic permits of growing vines successfully on almost flat ground, as, thanks to the constant westerly winds, they never lack proper aeration. In the valley of the Douro, where the summer heat is very great, the grapes have to be grown on high mountain slopes so that they may get all the aeration which they require to attain perfection.

The altitude and aspect of a vineyard are of greater importance than its latitude and longitude. In the sun-scorched valley of the Douro, for instance, vineyards may be planted at high altitudes on slopes facing north, north-west or south-west. On the other hand, in the colder valleys of the Moselle and of the Rhine, all the best vineyards will be found on moderate heights, chiefly facing south or south-east.

The vineyards of Rudesheim are said to owe their origin to the Emperor Charlemagne, who, whilst staying at Bingen in the early spring, noticed that the snow had melted away on the opposite bank of the Rhine, whilst it was still quite hard where he was. He forthwith ordered vines to be planted there, where they have thrived ever since. After Bingen, however, the Rhine takes a sharp turn to the north, with the result that, immediately to the north of Rudesheim, and on the same side, the same vines, planted in the same soil, and cultivated in exactly the same

way, will never yield wines of the same
excellence as those grown from Rudesheim to Hochheim, with a south-eastern
aspect.

As different kinds of soils suit different
kinds of vines, different climates, aspects
and altitudes are more or less suitable
to certain species of vines. Some varieties
will grow to perfection in the warm climate
of Sicily, but will only give poor results
in the South of France, and will not grow
in Germany. There are vines which like
the crest of wind-swept hills, and others
which require sheltered positions ; some
will thrive in reclaimed marshes, as on the
banks of the Gironde, in the *Palus* ; others
are only suited for hillside growing at
moderate altitudes, even while the soil,
climate and aspect are otherwise favourable. In Burgundy, for instance, all the
fine growths are planted in Pinot vines
at an altitude which only varies from 650
to 800 feet ; but on the same hill—in the
white grapes district for instance—the
upper part is planted in Aligoté, a species
of vine which never can have too much
air, but cannot bear humidity ; the middle

of the hill will be planted with the Pinot
Blanc Coulard and the lower part with the
Melon, a more common type of vine which
is not liable to the *coulure*, and which,
when its buds have been destroyed by
spring frosts, will produce fresh ones. If
the order were reversed, the *coulure* would
render the Pinots fruitless, the lack of
moisture would render the Melon grapes
hard and juiceless, and the excess of humidity would cripple the growth of the Aligoté.

Whoever has learnt at least the rudiments
of music, must know that C E G or D F A,
although different, are equally right chords,
but that C F G, D E G or any other such
combination would jar painfully on the
ear. In exactly the same way, perfect
grapes can only be produced where there
is a perfectly harmonious accord of three
elements—the right species of vine grown
on the right kind of soil and at the right
place, which comprehends climate, aspect
and altitude.

WEATHER

When, however, nature, the art of man
and the experience of many generations

have made it possible to happily arrive at the most perfect harmony between species, soil and aspect, the quality and quantity of the grapes the vine-grower may hope to gather are still and always must remain very uncertain, on account of that ever unknown factor, the weather.

The danger of spring frosts and the damage done by hailstorms may be minimised at the cost of much labour, trouble and expenditure, but there are neither scientific methods nor wealth capable of checking excessive rains or prolonged droughts. To the differences in the weather from year to year may be ascribed the differences often so striking and always noticeable between the produce of the same vineyards, but of different vintages.

The question of the weather is of paramount importance at the four most critical epochs of the growth of the vine, viz., the budding season in March or April, the flowering season in May or June (sometimes in July); the fruiting time in September or October and the wood-ripening season in October or November.

Frosts, in the spring, may destroy all hopes of a crop in the autumn ; excessive rains or winds may carry away the pollen of the flowers and prevent the fruit from setting ; the lack or the excess of rain or heat may interfere with the development and proper ripening of the grapes ; moist and mild weather in the late autumn may prevent the wood of the vines from ripening properly and thus handicap severely the crop of the following year.

Some good wine may be made from grapes which are over-ripe but never from unripe grapes. Generally speaking, however, the most important condition required of the grapes for the making of good wine is that they shall be sound and fully ripe. Unripe grapes contain a large percentage of acidity and very little glucose or sugar ; gradually, however, the acidity decreases and the glucose increases as the fruit is ripening under the summer sun, until it is quite ripe ; the quantity of glucose in the grape juice then remains stationary for a few days during which the acidity further decreases, without however, ever entirely disappearing. The grape is then ready to be plucked and made to yield its precious blood.

The more glucose there is in the ripe grape, the more alcohol the wine made therefrom will contain, and as the sun produces the glucose, it follows that the same vines which produce a thin wine, with an excess of acidity, after a cold and wet summer, will yield a bigger wine, with perchance a lack of acidity, after a hot and dry season.

The weather is, therefore, responsible to a large extent not only for the quantity of fruit the vine will bear, but also for the degree of excellence to which the grapes, and ultimately the wine, may attain.

It is not, however, one of the least remarkable features of this remarkable plant, the vine, that the excellence of its fruit, the grape, and consequently of the wine made therefrom, is greater where it suffers most from the vagaries of the weather. In the Argentine, for instance, where there is always sufficient heat to ripen the grapes, and where the vines are supplied with all the water they can require through a thorough system of irrigation ; in Algeria,

California, and at the Cape, where the climate is so much more reliable than in France or Germany, the vines yield a greater abundance of wine than in the Côte d'Or, the Médoc, the Marne or on the Rhine, but never of such fine quality. In all the best districts of France and Germany, there are rarely more than three good vintages in ten, but the quality of the wine made in a good year and the prices such wine will fetch, are very superior to those of the wines from vineyards which enjoy finer and more reliable weather.

CULTURE

Independently of species, soil, aspect and weather, the quality and quantity of fruit the vine will produce depend on the mode of cultivation. It may be laid down as a general rule that quantity is always obtained at the expense of quality, and the vine-grower must make up his mind which of the two will pay him best, which of the two his vineyard is better suited for, and adopt methods of cultivation accordingly.

There are, however, certain rules of

viticulture which apply to all vines alike.

PLANTING AND PROPAGATING.—The vine is planted and propagated in a variety of ways, either by slips, layers, cuttings, eyes, or by budding and grafting; the depth at which the vines are planted depends chiefly on the nature of the soil and climate of the district, a foot-and-a-half being considered sufficient in the Champagne country, whereas three feet is more usual in the valley of the Douro, where the greater heat makes it imperative to give the roots a greater depth.

PRUNING.—The Vine must be limited in its production for the finest quality of fruit to be obtained, and pruning is a very important operation, which varies with the species of vines and the climate of each district. Generally speaking, however, it may be said that hard pruning is the rule when quality is of greater importance than quantity, as is the case when fine wines are concerned.

HOEING.—In the early spring and summer, the hoe has to be applied to loosen the surface of the soil and remove all the weeds.

STAKING.—The vine is a climbing shrub, which cannot support itself, and stakes are used for the purpose.

FEEDING AND TREATING.—Manure as nourishment for the roots is not all that is often required by the vine ; its many enemies, whether insects or fungoid growths, make it necessary to spray sulphur and sulphate of copper on the leaves to check the inroads of insect pests and diseases.

VINTAGING.—When the grapes have reached a sufficient degree of maturity, they are gathered as rapidly as possible and brought to the press, where they are crushed and made to yield their sweet juice before they have had time to get bruised or to rot.

Note 1.—The family of the *Ampelidaceæ* comprises ten principal branches, viz. :—

1. Genus Ampelocissus.	6. Genus Parthenocissus.
2. „ Pterisanthes.	7. „ Ampelopsis.
3. „ Clematicissus.	8. „ Rhoicissus.
4. „ Tetrastigma.	9. „ Cissus.
5. „ Landukia.	10. „ Vitis.

Note 2.—Asiatic Types.

1. Vitis Coignetiæ (Early Caplat)	-		- Japan.
2. „ Thumbergi	-	-	-	- „
3. „ Flexuosa	-	-	-	- „
4. „ Amurensis	-	-	-	- Amur River.
5. „ Romaneti	-	-	-	- China.
6. „ Pagnuccii	-	-	-	- „
7. „ Picifolia -	-	-	-	- „
8. „ Lanata -	-	-	-	- India.
9. „ Pedicellata	-	-	-	- Himalayas.
10. Spinovitis Davidi	-	-	-	- China.

Note 3.—American Types.

1. Labrusca	-	- (Linne) -	- Labruscæ.
2. Californica	-	- (Bentham)	- Labruscoidæ
3. Caribacæ -	-	- (De Candolle)	„
4. Coriacea -	-	- (Shuttleworth)	„
5. Candicans	-	- (Englemann) -	„
6. Lincecumii	-	- (Buckley)	- Æstivales.
7. Bicolor -	-	- (Lecomte)	- „
8. Æstivalis -	-	- (Michaux)	- „
9. Berandieri	-	- (Planchon)	Cinerascentes.
10. Cordifolia -	-	- (Michaux)	- „
11. Cinerea -	-	- (Englemann) -	„
12. Rupestris	-	- (Scheele)	- Rupestres.
13. Monticola	-	- (Buckley)	- „
14. Arizonica -	-	- (Englemann) -	„
15. Riparia -	-	- (Michaux)	- Ripariæ.
16. Rubra	-	- (Michaux)	- „

CHAPTER IV

The Art of Wine-Making

WINE-MAKING is an art which the genius of man discovered at the dawn of the world's history, and which has largely contributed to the well-being of mankind and to the growth of all arts ever since.

The distinctive character of every wine is due principally to the species of grapes from which it is made, to the geographical situation and to the geological formation of the vineyards where those grapes are grown, and to the more or less favourable weather conditions prevailing in different years. But the striking differences which exist between various kinds of wines, either dark or light in colour, still or sparkling, sweet or dry, are due to the manner and degree in which they are fermented, and to the

way they are treated during and after
fermentation, or, in other words, to different methods of vinification.

The art of wine-making comprises
three principal stages : (1) the crushing
of the ripe grapes to obtain the must ;
(2) the fermenting of the must to obtain
wine ; and (3) the maturing of the wine
either in cask or bottle, constantly and
carefully watching it and attending to it,
before it is ready for consumption.

Methods of vinification, however, vary
according to each wine-producing district, and according to the finest type of
wine which the grapes, soil and climatic
conditions of different vine-growing districts
make it possible to obtain. If grapes
grown in the Douro valley, for instance,
were pressed, fermented and treated in
exactly the same way as grapes are pressed,
fermented and treated in the Champagne district, wine would be obtained
which would be neither Champagne nor
Port, and which would be very much
worse that the worst Champagne or the
worst Port. The same disastrous result
would be obtained by attempting to

introduce in the Champagne district wine-making methods which give excellent results at Oporto.

Whilst various processes of vinification obtain in different wine-producing districts, there is one all-important factor in the art of wine-making which is common to all, viz., fermentation.

FERMENTATION

Ours is a wonderful age! In every branch of science, remarkable progress has been made, whilst board schools and the daily press have, to a large extent, banished from the land both crass ignorance and true learning. The Socialist tub-thumper, the little shopman's son who has blossomed out into a suburban medical practitioner with a modest Scotch degree, and thousands of others with a superficial knowledge of a great many things and a really astounding amount of confidence in their own intellect, will tell you that old faiths and beliefs are fading away before the searchlight of modern science. Please, do not believe them. Ask them for a rational explanation of the phenomenon of fermentation, and the most learned amongst them will have to own their ignorance. Over thirty centuries ago, the Egyptians knew how, when and where vines grew and grape-juice became wine, but they could never tell the reason why. We know little or no more to-day, nor can any one of us understand or explain how some corn found in one of the Pharaohs' tombs grew and bore fruit when planted over here after twenty-two centuries of rest. The forces of Nature which surround us are beyond our intellect; we can note and observe them with the help of wonderful mechanical contrivances and greatly magnifying glasses; we can even more or less accurately describe them; but we never can explain them; we cannot ever get at the "Reason Why," that incessant, instinctive, haunting craving for knowledge of the cause and reason of things, a craving which many of us still believe may be satisfied in another and better world.

When grapes are crushed or pressed, their juice is sweet and watery, but, if left alone a little time, it will become turbid and boil spontaneously ; it then gradually simmers down, and eventually becomes not only perfectly still but also quite clear. The same liquid will then be found to be no longer sweet, but to contain alcohol.

The grape-juice is *must* before it begins to boil ; it becomes *wine* after it has ceased to boil. This is what we know as the phenomenon of fermentation, from the Latin *fervere*—to boil.

The cause of fermentation has been the object of many speculations in olden times, and of searching scientific investigations since the end of the eighteenth century. Lavoisier, the founder of modern chemistry, Gay-Lussac, Chaptal, and a very large number of French, German, English, Dutch and Italian chemists propounded theories of their own, which, however, failed to be really convincing. Then came the celebrated Liebig, whose theory, chiefly based on the works of Willis and Stahl, that fermentation was a purely chemical phenomenon, was accepted as final for many years. Pasteur, however, proved that Liebig was wrong, and that fermentation was due entirely to the presence of very active microscopic living organisms. This theory has been accepted also as final for the last forty years, but Buckner and others have now proved that Pasteur and Liebig were both wrong, and that the truth—the real, final truth!—is a compromise between the theories of these two great men.

We have neither the wish nor the time, however, to go deeply into the merits and demerits of various theories of fermentation, although it is a highly interesting subject (¹). Whether the cause of fermentation be of a purely chemical nature or due to living yeast cells, or to a combination of both causes, it is sufficient for us to know that a molecule of grape sugar is transformed by fermentation into two molecules of alcohol, two molecules of carbon dioxide, and some minute quantities of glycerine and other matters.

It is also known that cold retards and

(¹). For the latest scientific theory of fermentation, see the 1911 Edition of Jorgensen's *Micro-organisms and Fermentation.*

heat excites fermentation, which, however, ceases altogether either when the
liquid is brought to boiling point or contains too great a proportion of alcohol.
The sweeter the must, the more alcohol
there will be in the wine, up to a point ;
for when the fermentation has transformed a certain quantity of the grape-
sugar into alcohol, or when alcohol is added
to the fermenting must, whatever quantity of grape-sugar may be left in the
liquid will remain unfermented as soon as
the proportion of alcohol contained therein
is such as to check all further fermentation.

BLENDING

After fermentation, the most important
factor in the art of wine-making is blending.

There are many people who, without
having ever really given the matter any
consideration, think that the blending of
wines or spirits savours of adulteration ;
they argue that, although it may be permitted by law, it cannot be absolutely
right nor honest since it is only resorted to
in order to pass off wines and spirits which
it would be certainly more difficult, and

perhaps even impossible to sell if they were not blended. Such a notion is not only erroneous but even ridiculous, for should a similar argument be carried to its logical conclusion in any other field of human art or industry, we should have to condemn every progress and improvement as a tampering with the laws of Nature.

The blending of wines from different vineyards or of different years has a two-fold object : firstly and chiefly to obtain better and more regular quality, and secondly, to reduce the average cost of production.

If there are two types of wine more popular in this country than any other, they are Port and Champagne, and Ports and Champagnes, with only very few exceptions, are always blended ; so that it cannot be said that blending only applies to the cheaper and commoner sorts of wines. With the exception of the fine growths of the Gironde, Burgundy, Germany and Hungary, practically all the other wines either are blended or could be improved by judicious blending.

When a wine lacks acidity, for instance,

and another suffers from an excess of acidity, it stands to reason that by blending the two together a much more palatable wine will be obtained. Both these wines may be the produce of the same vineyard but of different years, or else of different vineyards, more or less favourably situated in the same district ; the price may be very much higher one year than another or in one part of a certain district than anywhere else in the same region. Intelligent blending of wines is the only natural and rational way of correcting the faults of two or three or more imperfect wines and of thus creating a type as near perfection as possible or as near the standard of excellence which is aimed at and which will have to be maintained year after year.

Delicate and difficult as the trade in wines is, it would be considerably more difficult, not to say impracticable, were it not that shippers are able, thanks to the art of blending, to maintain the standard of quality and the average cost of their wines as uniform as possible, in spite of the vagaries of the weather from year to year.

Blending is an operation which requires considerable experience, judgment and intelligence; it is absolutely legitimate, and moreover, it is the only natural and honest way of improving, and, in many cases, rendering more lasting the majority of wines.

Let us now rapidly examine the different modes of vinification which are responsible for the making of still and sparkling, dry and sweet, red and white wines.

STILL WINES: RED

(a) FRANCE

When the grapes are fully ripe, but not over-ripe, the gathering takes place with great care and rapidity. The bunches are cut, and every green, rotten, or otherwise unsound berry is immediately removed and thrown into a special receptacle; all the perfectly sound bunches are then placed in baskets which, when full, are carried to the road, where a cart is waiting with a vat, into which the baskets are emptied. The vat being full, it is taken to the *celliers* and emptied into presses, where the grapes are crushed. The crushed grapes, juice, skins, pips, and stalks are then transferred to large wooden tubs, where they are left alone until the first force of the fermentation, which soon afterwards sets in, has completely spent itself. After a few days, the newly-made wine is drawn from the fermenting vats into hogsheads, where the fermentation still goes on at a much quieter rate for some time to come.

During the year which follows the vintage, the new wines are racked, *i.e.*, separated from their lees and drawn into fresh casks, at least three times; they are further racked during succeeding years according to the nature and style of the wines produced in different vineyards and in different years. The red wines of Bordeaux, Burgundy, Beaujolais, and all those made in a like manner, can claim to be perfectly natural; they are fermented thoroughly and without any outside help or hindrance; the art of man only intervenes to remove every possible cause of imperfection, but not to assist or hamper Nature. In order to obtain the best must, all imperfect

berries are carefully removed when the
grapes are picked, and in order to avoid
the wine acquiring from its lees too
pungent a taste, which might hide its
finer bouquet, it is racked from time to
time, but nothing is added to either the
must or wine to improve its colour, body,
flavour, or alcoholic strength, all of
which are due to the natural process
of fermentation.

Whether in the Médoc or the Graves
district, at Hermitage or in the Côte
d'Or, red wines are made on the same
principle, and the differences which
exist between the wines of Bordeaux
and those of Burgundy, and even between
those of Margaux and Haut-Brion, are
due to the species of vines and the
nature of the soil, aspect and elevation
of such vineyards, far more than to slight
differences in the methods of vinification obtaining in different districts. As
regards all the fine growths of either
the Bordelais or the Côte d'Or, the
wines made from the grapes gathered
on each separate estate or vineyard are
never blended together in good years,

as each should possess sufficient excellence of itself not to require the
addition of any other wine, even if
made from vines grown in the immediate neighbourhood. Besides, if a
Château Lafite, an Ausone, a Clos de
Vougeot, a Romanée Conti, or any other
such wine, were ever blended with
other wines of even similar excellence,
they would lose at once their own
characteristic bouquet and taste to
which they owe their greatest charm
and value. On the other hand, if 70
tuns of wine are made one year on the
Château Brane Cantenac Estate, for
instance, these 70 tuns will be identical
in every respect ; all the grapes cannot
have been gathered nor all the wine
made on the same day, but all the produce of the Château Brane Cantenac
Estate will be blended together, as soon
as the new wine is drawn from the
fermenting vats, so as to ensure complete
uniformity of quality.

After being left in casks a certain
number of years, red wines are bottled
and go on improving in glass for a

more or less considerable period, which
greatly varies with every different wine
and vintage. As a general rule, it may
be said that a red wine has not reached
the age limit when it will begin to
deteriorate, so long as it retains its
" fruit," the natural softness and sweetness
of the grape. After a time, however,
this disappears, and the tannin asserts
itself; the wine then becomes hard and
unpleasantly dry; it is on the down-
grade and has been kept too long.

(b) PORTUGAL

In the valley of the Douro, there is no
Clos de Vougeot, Château Margaux or
Johannisberg, no special unique vineyard having attained a world-wide fame,
the produce of which is absolutely
distinct from any other wine grown
in the same district. In each farm or
quinta, the grapes are gathered when
ripe and brought to the *lagars*. These
are large, square stone troughs which,
when filled with grapes, are entered by
a number of bare-legged men who dance
and jump about to the tune of much

music and song until the whole lagar is
a mass of discoloured husks in a purple
sea of liquid. This is left alone in the
lagars for three or four days until the
first or tumultuous fermentation has
spent its force; the new wine is then
drawn into large wooden vessels where the
fermentation goes on at a slower rate.
When a certain proportion of the grape
sugar has been transformed into alcohol
by fermentation, some brandy distilled
from the wine of the country is added to
the fermenting wine; it raises the alcoholic degree to such an extent that
fermentation ceases at once, and a large
proportion of the grape sugar contained
in the must is left unfermented in its
natural state. From each quinta, the
new wines are then carted to the Douro
and sent down to Oporto, where they
are blended and stored in very extensive
warehouses or lodges. Once that stage
reached, the Port wine shippers have to
decide whether the new wines have to
be shipped as vintage wines or not. In
the first instance, the wines are sent over
here a year or two after being made,

I

and are bottled soon after. Slowly does
the wine thus bottled go on improving,
the added brandy losing some of its fire
and feeding upon some of the original
grape-sugar left in the wine to combine
with it and form that captivating and
generous wine we all know as fine old
vintage Port. But, if instead of being
bottled soon after the vintage, the new
wines are allowed to age and mature
in cask in the Oporto Lodges, undis-
turbed for many years, the colour will sink
into the wood of the cask, the brandy
will lose some of its strength, and the
outcome will be what we know as tawny
port, a wine lighter in colour and
body, but more easily digested, very
luscious and fascinating.

The red wines of Bordeaux and of
Oporto are the two principal types of
still red wines, the former dry and
light, the latter sweet and heavier. All
the dry natural wines made in every
part of the world are to all intents and
purposes made upon the same principles as at Bordeaux; the must is
thoroughly and naturally fermented.

All the other sweet red wines made in other countries are also made on the same principles as obtain in the valley of the Douro, the fermentation of the must being arrested by the addition of brandy.

STILL WINES: WHITE

(a) FRANCE AND GERMANY

The juice of practically all grapes, whether black or white, is greenish white, and the colouring matter resides in the skins. White wines, therefore, may be made from black grapes in presses which retain skins, pips and stalks, whilst the juice runs away immediately into a separate tub or vat. Most white wines, however, are made from white grapes, the juice of which is fermented either with or without the husks. After the first fermentation, which takes place soon after the pressing, as in the case of red wines, the newly-made and still fermenting wine is drawn into smaller casks, and racked from time to time, and even sometimes fined before being racked to ensure greater limpidity.

The majority of the white wines of France and Germany are dry; that is to say, the whole of the grape sugar contained in their must is transformed into alcohol and carbonic acid gas after a year or so. There are, however, some white wines made in the Sauternes district which are distinctly sweet, although quite as natural as the driest Chablis or Moselle wine. The sweetness which is such a characteristic of the Sauternes wines made in good years is due to the species of vines grown in that district, and to the fact that the grapes they produce, when fully ripe, can be left to partly shrivel in the sun without rotting and becoming useless, as most grapes would. It is true that, once the full degree of maturity has been reached, the quantity of glucose contained in the berries no longer increases, but the acidity further decreases and some of the water in each berry is absorbed by the stalks, so that it is not the actual quantity but the relative

amount of grape sugar contained in each
berry which has increased to a large
extent. When such grapes are pressed,
the quantity of must obtained is naturally very much smaller than if they
had been crushed as soon as they had
reached their full maturity ; the amount
of grape sugar would have been the
same then, but the quantity of water
and the acidity would have been greater.

The excess of grape-sugar contained
in the must obtained from such over-
ripe grapes is such, that fermentation
cannot use it all, and it adds to the
wine that luscious fruitiness which is
as incomparable as it is natural.

In the Bavarian Palatinate, where Riesling and Traminer vines are grown close to
the soil and heavily manured, white wines
are also made which possess a remarkable and perfectly natural sweetness,
entirely due to the excess of grape-sugar
contained in the must, whenever the
summer has been favourable.

Most white wines, whether sweet or
dry, which are produced in all other vine-
growing countries, are made practically

in the same way as we have here briefly
indicated.

(b) SPAIN

The methods of vinification which
obtain in the south of Spain are very
different from those of any other vine-
growing country.

In the best districts, the gathering of
the grapes is done very carefully by going
over the vineyards several times and only
cutting those bunches which have attained to perfect maturity. Once picked,
the grapes are first of all laid on straw
mats for several hours, after which they
are placed in a wooden " lagar," a receptacle about ten feet square and raised
some three feet from the ground. The
lagar being full, the grapes are trodden
by men with wooden shoes, and the juice
runs out immediately into large butts
which are stored in the cellars or *bodegas*,
where it goes on fermenting for some
months. Towards the end of November,
the new wines having fallen more or less
bright, the expert tasters begin their all-
important duties, which consist chiefly

in classifying each butt according to the quality or style of wine it is found to contain. In one and the same cellar the wines made from the same vineyards in September may all possess some different characteristic in the following November. This is due chiefly to the way each butt has been affected by a more or less rapid and thorough fermentation, and the expert tasters have to decide what amount of wine spirit is to be added to each butt; they must, furthermore, determine into which category and to which degree of excellence in each category the wine of each butt is to be placed.

The three principal classes of fine sherries are the *Fino*, a wine of very pale colour and delicate fragrance; the *Amontillado*, a wine which requires to be kept longer to acquire its distinctive character and which derives its name from the town of Montilla; and the *Oloroso*, a full nutty wine darker in colour.

In each of these three main classes of sherries, there are many varieties and degrees of excellence. The aim of each shipper, however, is to maintain the style and quality of each type of the wines he has to ship at various prices. This is done by the process of blending wines of different years, a system known as *Solera*, from the word *suelo*, ground, taken in the sense of basis or formation.

Sweet wines are also made in the south of Spain, some by the process of allowing the ripe Pedro Jimenez grapes to dry partly in the sun on straw mats before being pressed, and others by adding wine-spirit at 66 o.p. to the newly pressed grape-juice or must, which is thus prevented from fermenting. The former is known as " Pedro Jimenez " wine, and the latter, which it is possible to produce at a much smaller cost, is called " Dulce Apagado." There is also a sweet wine made in the same way as the Pedro Jimenez, but with Muscat grapes, which is known as sweet " Muscatel."

SPARKLING WINES

Fermentation transforms grape-juice into alcohol and carbonic acid gas ; this process goes on for a short time at a very rapid pace, and then for many months

at a very much slower rate. The alcohol
stays in the wine, and the carbonic acid
gas loses itself in the air. To keep part
of this carbonic acid gas in the wine is
the chief feature of the art of sparkling
wine making.

Champagne is the first of all sparkling
wines, in point of antiquity and of importance, and all the sparkling wines
which are now made in every wine-producing country of the world, are made
according to the Champagne methods,
which are chiefly as follows :

As soon as the grapes—which in the
Champagne district are mostly black
grapes—are ripe, they are gathered with
extreme care, all unsound berries being re-
jected. Placed in large square oak presses,
the grapes are pressed as soon as they
are picked and always close to the vineyards whence they come, as they are too
tender to bear transporting any distance.
After the first fermentation has taken
place in vats which hold a " pressing,"
about 2,000 litres or 440 gallons, the
newly-made wines are drawn into hogsheads which are taken to the cellars,

where they will be left to ferment un-
disturbed until the cold weather sets in;
the fermentation is then momentarily
arrested or greatly checked by the cold
and all the sediment falls to the bottom
of the cask; the new wines are then
racked and blended. Each particular
growth possesses certain characteristics,
and it is only by judicious blending of the
produce of different growths that perfection can be obtained. In the spring
which follows the vintage, the fermentation, which has been much slower during
the winter, becomes more active. The
amount of grape-sugar left in the new
wines is then tested, and it is possible
to know exactly how much work is left
for the fermentation to perform and the
exact quantity of alcohol and carbonic
acid gas yet to be produced. The new
wines are then bottled, tightly and securely
corked and laid to rest. The fermentation still goes on inside the bottle as it
did inside the casks, but the carbonic
acid gas produced can no longer escape
and it remains in the wine. After being
bottled a certain time, the wine ceases

to ferment and contains its maximum
quantity of alcohol, the proportion of
carbonic acid gas corresponding to the
amount of sugar left at the bottling time,
and a good deal of sediment produced by
the process of fermentation and ageing.   If
it were not for this sediment the wine
would then be ready for consumption,
but it cannot be allowed to leave the cellar
until it is absolutely " star bright."   To
arrive at this result, the bottles are placed
in specially-made perforated tables, neck
downwards ; they are then given a long
series of twists and shakes which make
the sediment fall upon the cork and settle
there ; when this is done, the cork is
removed very rapidly and in such a way
that all the sediment which had settled
on it is expelled with as little loss of wine
as possible. It only remains to cork it
again securely and the wine is then ready
for consumption, both sparkling and
bright—a fully and naturally fermented
wine. After the wine has been freed from
the sediment it contained, and before
corking it again, some sweet syrup is
sometimes added to sweeten sparkling

wines. This is done, however, only to suit the taste of some consumers who like and demand a sweetened sparkling wine.

It has been quite impossible to do more in one short chapter than to briefly indicate the principal methods of vinification which are responsible for the marked differences existing between various types of well-known wines. One cannot do justice within such narrow bounds to so important a subject, the study of which cannot help to convince one that, whilst the vine is a naturally fruitful tree, and whilst fermentation is one of Nature's own laws, the excellence, the abundance, and the variety of the wines we know and enjoy, are due to the intelligence, to the ingenuity, and to the industry of man, and to the noble art of wine-making.

CHAPTER V

The Art of Distillation

1.—Historical

THE art of distillation, taken in its most comprehensive sense, was known to the Ancients who distilled sea-water and certain perfumes. But the process of distillation does not appear to have been applied to wine before the end of the eleventh century, when a certain Marcus Græcus gave us the earliest known recipe for the distillation of Aqua Ardens or Ardent Water, in a manuscript entitled *Liber ignium ad comburendos hostes*, now in the Bibliothèque Nationale, Paris, under the Nos. 7156 and 7158.

A certain Doctor Albucasis, who lived at Cordoba, in Spain, during the twelfth century, has also left us a detailed description of the distilling apparatus then in use for the distillation of rose water and of wine.

In the thirteenth century, R. Lulli, in his *Theatrum Chemicum*, and Arnaud de Villeneuve, in his treatise *De Vinis*, show us that the distillation of wine had then been placed on a more scientific basis, and that the virtues of distilled wine were beginning to be appreciated. " Some people call it Eau de Vie," wrote Arnaud de Villeneuve, " and this name is remarkably suitable, since it is really a water of immortality. Its virtues are beginning to be recognised, it prolongs life, clears away ill-humours, revives the heart and maintains youth."

At that early period, distillers were so much impressed with the marvellous qualities of distilled wine that they imagined it contained some of the attributes of the fire which had helped to make it. They sought to prolong distillation as much as possible, on heated sand, and they endeavoured to let the contact between the liquid in the still and the heat of the fire be as long as possible, thinking that such was the surest means of obtaining a more fiery spirit.

During the fourteenth century, much progress was made in the art of distillation, both in France and Germany, and wine spirit was used medicinally and sold by apothecaries at prices which were then considered prohibitive.

In 1307, an entry in the account book of the Comtesse Mahaut reads thus :— " For wine bought by Girard to make burning water of, for our daughter, ten sous and ten deniers."

In 1358, in his *Pratica Alchimica*, Ortholaus gives very exact directions for the distillation of wine, and for rectifying the spirit obtained first.

From the publication, at Augsburg, in 1483, of a treatise by Michel Schreik, *Verzeichniss der Ausgebranden Wasser*, and, at Bamberg, in 1493, of a poem dealing with the merits and demerits of alcohol, it is evident that, in Germany the use of spirits was, during the fifteenth century, no longer restricted to medicinal purposes.

In 1496, the municipality of Nurem-
berg was already taking measures to
check the abuse of spirits, a decree
issued that year forbidding " the sale of
distilled waters on Sundays and other
holidays, in private houses, as well as
by druggists and other merchants, in
their shops, in the market, in the street,
or elsewhere, so as to put a stop to their
abuse and excessive consumption."

Liquids fermented from grain appear
to have been first distilled on a large
scale in the fifteenth century, and it
was due to this fact that the consumption of spirits rapidly became
more general, particularly so in Northern
Europe, where wine was comparatively
expensive and out of the reach of the
majority of the people.

Ever since, the consumption of spirits
has grown more popular and more
considerable all the world over, whilst
the industrial utilisation of alcohol has
opened a practically unlimited field to
the energies of the distiller.

Aqua Vitæ does not appear to have
enjoyed any popularity in England

before the sixteenth century. Some knowledge of the art of distillation may have been brought to this country by Raymond Lulli, during the reign of Edward III. The inventor of the *Universal Art* had great faith in "the marvaylous use and comoditie of burning waters even in warres, a little before the joining of batayle, to styr and encourage the souldiours' mindes." No record has been found, however, to show that distilled spirits were consumed in England before the sixteenth century, although they were commonly used in Ireland, and probably also in Scotland at a much earlier date.

In 1525, a translation of Jerome Braunschweig's important work on distillation was published in London, under the title of *The Vertuose Boke of Distyllacyon of the Waters of all maner of Herbes*, "for the help and profit of surgeons, physicians, pothecaries, and all manner of people." This seems to have been the earliest book of any importance, in this country, published with a view of rendering the science of

K

distillation more popular. The *Vertuose Boke* bestows great praises on *Aqua Vitæ*, the use of which, however, was chiefly recommended medicinally. " Aqua Vitæ," according to the *Vertuose Boke*, " is commonly called the mistress of all medicines, for it easeth the diseases coming from cold. It giveth also young courage in a person, and causeth him to have a good memory and remembrance. It purifyeth the five wits of melancholy and of all uncleanliness, when it is drunk by reason and measure; that is to understand five or six drops in the morning, fasting, with a spoonful of wine . . . . . . it comforteth the heart and causeth a body to be merry, etc."

In 1559, when Peter Morwyng published his *Treasure of Evonymous*, wine was no longer distilled solely by apothecaries for medicinal purposes. There were already a certain number of distillers in London, whose trade consisted in distilling spirits from wine-lees and unsound wine obtained at very low prices from the vintners and coopers, a practice which Morwyng does not find fault with. "Burning water or Aqua Vitæ," he writes, "is drawn oute of wyne, but, wyth us, out of the wyne lies (*sic*) only, specially of them that sel it, and by this onely almost get their livying. And peradventure it is never a whit the worse that it is drawne oute of lees ; for Lullus teacheth that it may be wel destilled of corrupt wine, yea, if it be distilled often it shal be made the more effectuall (that is to say) hotter and drier, etc."

The rapidity with which the popularity of the crude, home-made spirits spread in England is evidenced by the numerous editions of the works on distillation. Two editions of the *Treasure of Evonymous* were printed in 1559 ; a little later, another treatise on the same subject by Conrad Gesner and translated by George Baker, was published under the title of the *Newe Jewell of Health*, and the demand was so great that several editions had to be issued within a short space of time.

In the *Jewell of Health*, we read

that good wine was sometimes used
for distillation, but the process was
then considered very wasteful. " The
burning water, or water of life, is
sometimes distilled out of pleasant and
good wine, as the white or the red,
but oftener out of the wine lees of a
certain eager-savour or corrupt Wine.

" Further, when out of pure wine a
water of life is distilled, I hear that
out of a great quantity of good wine,
a little yield or quantity of burning
water is to be distilled, but out of the
lees of wine, a much (greater) yield
and quantity (are) gathered."

It was not, however, until the reign
of Elizabeth and after the expedition
to the Low Countries in 1585, that
the taste for spirits became prevalent
in England amongst the lower classes.

The taste for strong liquor and fiery
spirits appears to have made rapid
progress in England during the
seventeenth century; the distillation
of home-made spirits was repeatedly
encouraged by legislation, and it
soon attained considerable importance,

whilst the imports of brandy, rum and arrack increased very rapidly during the same period. Rum from the West Indies and arrack from the East were not imported until the close of the seventeenth century, and, even then, in insignificant quantities only. Brandy from Bordeaux, Rochelle or Nantes, Spain, Portugal and even from the Canaries, was the staple foreign spirit, whilst Aqua Vitæ and strong waters were chiefly supplied from wine-lees or strong ale distilled in England and flavoured with spices or other ingredients.

Previous to the reign of Charles I., there does not appear to have existed any control whatever over the manufacture of spirits in England; everybody was then free to distil spirits from whatever source he pleased and in whichever way he chose. This liberty was undoubtedly the cause of much unpalatable and unwholesome trash being sold as spirits, which had been distilled from sour wine dregs or putrid beer-wash. It was in order to prevent as far as possible the manufacture and sale of

such injurious products that Charles I.
granted the first Charter of the Distillers
Company, in 1638. The person who
seems to have been primarily instrumental
in promoting the movement for the incorporation of the Distillers was Sir
Theodore de Mayern, physician to the
King. In conjunction with Dr. Thomas
Cademan, medical adviser to the Queen,
and the first Master of the Distillers
Company, Mayern prepared a series of
regulations and bye-laws for the manage-
ment of the new scheme, which were
published in 1639 under the following
title :—

" The Distiller of London : Compiled and set forth
by the Special Licence and Command of the King's
Most Excellent Majesty. For the sole use of the
Company of Distillers of London. And by them to
be duly observed and practised."

To protect the public from unwholesome spirit it was decreed :

" That no Afterworts or Wash (made by Brewers,
etc.) called Blew John, nor musty unsavoury or
unwholesome tills, or dregs of beer or ale ; nor unwholesome or adulterated wines, or Lees of Wines,
nor unwholesome sugar-waters ; musty unsavoury or
unwholesome returned beer or ale ; nor rotten corrupt
or unsavoury fruits, druggs, spices, herbs, seeds ; nor

any other ill-conditioned materials of what kind soever, shall henceforth be distilled, extracted or drawn into small spirits, or low wines, or be any other ways used, directly or indirectly, by any of the Members of this Company, or their successors at any time hereafter for ever."

The regulations enacted by the Distillers Company failed to ensure greater purity in English-made spirits because the Company never enjoyed any of the trading monopolies which alone would have made it possible to control the conduct of the trade. Charles II., James II., and William III., encouraged the distillation of home grain, in order to promote agriculture, allowing every Englishman to distil spirits from English-grown corn. The most important measure passed by Parliament to that effect was the Act of II. William and Mary, which begins :

"An Act for the encouraging the distillation of brandy and spirits from corn. First, the trade and commerce of France being prohibited, and all their goods from being imported in the kingdom ; And whereas good and wholesome brandy, aqua vitæ, and spirits may be drawn and made from malted corn ; For the encouragement therefore of the making of brandy, strongwaters, and spirits from malted corn, and for the greater consumption of corn and the advantage of tillage in this kingdom. The King, Queen and Parliament then assembled have thus ordained it. . . ."

In 1673, a petition was presented to Parliament, praying that the importation of brandy, coffee, mum (a strong ale brewed chiefly from wheat malt), tea and chocolate might be prohibited on the ground that these beverages greatly hindered the consumption of barley, malt and wheat, products of the land ; and the petition went on to say :

" Before brandy which is now become common and sold in every little alehouse, came over into England in such quantities as it now doth, we drank good strong beer and ale, and all laborious people (which are far the greatest part of the kingdom), their bodies requiring, after hard labour, some strong drink to refresh them did therefore every morning and evening used to drink a pot of ale or a flagon of strong beer, which greatly promoted the consumption of our own grain, and did them no great prejudice ; it hindered not their work, neither did it take away their senses nor cost them much money, whereas (the petition continued) the prohibition of brandy would . . . prevent the destruction of His Majesty's subjects, many of whom have been killed by drinking thereof, it not agreeing with their constitution."

In 1684, the whole of English-made

spirits on which excise was paid amounted to 527,000 gallons, whilst there were 202 tuns, 36 pieces, and 19 casks, equal to about 29,000 gallons of foreign spirits imported in London during the month of February, 1683.

In 1694, the produce of all the stills in England amounted to 1,885,752 gallons of low-wines, or 754,300 gallons of spirits. In the same year, in spite of the prohibition of French spirits, there were imported from Holland, Spain, Portugal and the Canaries, in the port of London alone, 706 tuns, 223 pipes, 425 casks, 70 hogsheads, 52 butts and 8 pipes of foreign brandy, about a million and a quarter gallons.

Home-made Aqua Vitæ had nothing in common with Brandy or distilled wine ; it was a spirit made from ale or the lees of wine and flavoured with a very great variety of herbs or roots. In his *English House-Wife*, Markham has the two following recipes for making " an excellent Aqua Vitæ : "

" Take of rosemary two handfulls, of marjerom, winter savory, rosemary, rue, unset time, germander,

ribwort, harts-tongue, mouseare, white wormwood,
bugloss, red sage, liver-wort, hoar-hound, fine lavender,
hyssop-crops, pennyroyal, 1 red fennell, of each of
these one handfull ; of elicampane roots, clean pared
and sliced, two handfulls; then take all these aforesaid
and shred them, but not wash them, then take four
gallons or more of strong ale, and one gallon of sack
lees, and put all these aforesaid herbs shred into it,
and then put into it one pound of lycoras bruised, half
a pound of aniseeds clean sifted and bruised, and of
mace and nutmegs bruised of each one ounce ; then
put altogether into your stilling pot, close covered
with rye paste, and make a soft fire under your pot,
and as the head of the limbeck heateth, draw out
your hot water and put in cold, keeping the head of
your limbeck still with cold water, but see that your
fire be not too rash at the first, but let your water
come at leisure, and take heed into your stilling, that
your water change not white ; for it is not so strong as
the first draught is ; and when the water is distilled,
take a gallon glass with a white mouth, and put therein
a pottle of the best water and clearest, and put into
it a pottle of *rosa solis*, and half a pound of dates
bruised, and one ounce of grains, and half a pound
of sugar, half a pound of seed pearl beaten, three
leaves of fine gold ; stir all these together well, then
stop your glass, and set it in the sun the space of one
or two months, and then chlarifie it, and use it at
your discretion, for a spoonfull or two at a time is
sufficient, and the vertues are infinite."

The second way indicated for making
an "excellent Aqua Vitæ" is not quite
so fantastic as the preceding, although

Markham might have more rightly said of both recipes " take it at your peril," than " at your discretion."

" Fill a pot with red wine, clean and strong, and put therein the powders of cammomile, jilley flowers, ginger, pellitory, nutmeg, gallengal, spicknard, quenebus, grains of pure long pepper, black pepper, cummin, fennel seed, smallage, parsley, sage, rue, mint, calamint, and horshow, of each of them a like quantity, and beware they differ not the weight of a dram under or above ; then put all the powders abovesaid into the wine, and after put them into the distilling pot, and distill it with a soft fire, and look that it be well luted about with rye paste, so that no fume or breath goe forth, and looke that the fire be temperate ; also receive the water out of the lymbeck into a glass vial. This water is called the water of life. . . ."

Then follow directions how to make *Aqua Composita*, distilled from " the best ale that can be brewed," the *Imperial Water*, from Gascony wine, *Cinamon Water*, from Sack, and " Six most precious waters " which are said to possess remarkable virtues.

Markham further indicates a few of the strong-waters which a provident house-wife should always keep in case of emergency.

" Therefore first I would have her furnish herself

of very good stills, for the distillation of all kinds of
waters, which stills would either be of tin, or sweet
earth, and in them she shall distil all sorts of waters
meet for the health of her household, as sage water,
which is good for all rheums, and collicks ; raddish
water, which is good for the stone ; angelica water,
good against infection ; celandine water for sore eyes ;
vine water, for itchings ; rosewater and eye-bright
water for dimme sights ; rosemary water for fistulæs ;
treacle water for mouth cankers ; water of cloves for
the pain in the stomach ; saxifrage water for gravell
and hard urine ; allom water for old ulcers, and a
world of others, any of which will last a full year at
least.   Then she shall know that the best waters for
the smoothing of the skin, and keeping the face
delicate and amiable, are those which are distilled,
from beanflowers, from strawberries, from vine leaves,
from goates-milk, from asses milk, from the whites of
eggs, from the flowers of lilies, from dragons, from
calves feet, from bran or from yelks of eggs, any of
which will last a year or better."

In the *Britannian Magazine* (1691)
W. Y. Worth tells us that "Aqua
Vitæ is nothing else but well brewed
beer, that is strongly hop'd and well
fermented" distilled and rectified; he
asserts that "Brandy" made from
beer, cider, perry or fruit wines is
"little inferiour to that of France,"
and he also gives full particulars for
the manufacture of strong-waters of

aniseed, caroway, cardamum, hearts-
ease, angelica, wormwood, mint, etc.

J. Lightbody, " Philomath," published
at about the same time a treatise on
brewing and distilling, entitled *Every
man his own gauger*, in which he gives
the recipe " to make the best sort of
Right Irish Usquebaugh," as follows :

" Take of good spirits, 12 gallons. Put therein
of aniseeds, nutmegs, sugar, carroway-seeds, of each
four ounces, distil the whole to proof spirit, put there-
to liquorish, raisins of the sun 2 pound, and 4 lb. of
sugar, let it drain through a flannel bag, and fine
it down with the whites of eggs and wheat floor.
This is the only way that natives of Ireland make
this liquor, which is approved of to exceed all the
other new ways of making it, being but imitations of
the original."

The more important the art of distillation became, the more attention it
received, both commercially and scientifically, with the result that many im-
provements were from time to time
introduced into former methods of distilling ; these have gradually been
perfected to such a degree that the
industry of distillation is now, in all
civilised countries, one of the most

important and one of the most profitable to State Exchequers.

11.—The Theory of Distillation

Strictly speaking, the art of distillation as applied to spirits, consists in
isolating, by heat, the different elements
of which any alcoholic liquid may be
composed.

The marked differences, however,
which exist between various potable
spirits are due, in the first instance, to
the differences existing between various
fermented liquids from which such
spirits are distilled, and, in the
second place, to different methods of
distillation.

It is by fermentation, not by distillation, that alcohol is obtained, so that
the first care of the distiller is to
obtain by fermentation the alcoholic
liquid he will have to distil.

What is alcohol ? Some call it a
food and others a poison ; some say
that it is a stimulant and others an
irritant ; some condemn its use and

many more praise it, but no one can possibly give a definition of alcohol which will be acceptable to all, no one but the chemist, who will tell you that alcohol is a compound of carbon, hydrogen and oxygen in certain proportions.

Chemists recognise 65 simple bodies, all others being compound bodies. A simple body is one which cannot be divided, and a compound body is one that is formed of a combination of two or more simple bodies. One may crush pure sulphur, for instance, or treat it by fire, water, electricity or acids without obtaining anything but sulphur ; Science is unable to sub-divide sulphur, and so it calls it a simple body. The same applies to carbon, oxygen, hydrogen, etc. On the other hand, water is a compound body, because it can be divided and can easily be proved to be a combination of two simple bodies, hydrogen and oxygen. In chemistry, hydrogen is known by the letter H, oxygen by the letter O, and carbon by the letter C. If water were a combination of one

part of hydrogen and one part of
oxygen, chemists would simply call it
HO ; but it so happens that the proportion of hydrogen to oxygen is as
two to one, so that water is designated
by H_2O. If we take away from water
—H_2O—one of its atoms of hydrogen
and replace it by a hydro-carbon
radical, that is to say a compound of
hydrogen and carbon, we shall obtain
different combinations of hydrogen,
carbon and oxygen, corresponding to
different types of alcohol. If, for
instance, we add a compound composed
of one atom of carbon and three of
hydrogen to HO, we shall have the
formula CH_3HO or CH_4O, a compound
body known as methyl alcohol or wood
alcohol. It we were to add to HO two
atoms of carbon and five of hydrogen,
we should have the formula C_2H_5HO
or C_2H_6O, which corresponds to ethyl
alcohol or wine alcohol. In the same
way, the formula of amyl alcohol or
fusel oil, is $C_5H_{11}HO$; that of propyl
alcohol C_3H_7HO ; that of butyl alcohol
C_4H_9HO, etc.

The member of the large family of alcohols which interests us most and the only one we shall deal with here is ethyl alcohol, a compound body consisting of two atoms or molecules of carbon, six molecules of hydrogen and one molecule of oxygen.

To make ethyl alcohol, therefore, it suffices to put together two molecules of carbon with six molecules of hydrogen and one molecule of oxygen. Theoretically, such a feat is possible, but practically it is not only difficult but also absolutely unnecessary, since that same combination is the natural result of alcoholic fermentation. Fermentation, as we know, is a phenomenon which transforms the sugar contained in the juice of the grape and produces principally carbonic acid gas and ethyl alcohol.

The juice of the grape ferments naturally and thus becomes wine, which was the first alcoholic liquid to be distilled, and for a long time the only one. Natural wines, however, never contain a large proportion of alcohol, so

L

that much wine must be burnt or
distilled to obtain a comparatively small
quantity of spirit. On the other hand,
climatic conditions render viticulture
perforcedly limited, so that the production of wine has never been greatly
in excess of the consumption thereof.
Both the short supply and the higher
cost of grape-spirit have thus placed
Brandy or distilled wine beyond the
reach of the masses in all but wine-
growing districts.

Had not the ingenuity of man discovered any other material to distil
except the naturally fermented juice of
the grape and of a few other fruits,
spirits would be as scarce now as in
the twelfth century, and much more
costly. As a matter of fact, grape
spirits are on the whole very much less
plentiful and very much dearer, whilst
their consumption is considerably smaller
than that of other spirits.

Grape juice contains natural yeast
and sugar, and the former, as we
know, transforms the latter into alcohol ;
if, therefore, we obtain by some direct

or indirect means a liquid containing
sugar, and if we add yeast to it, we
shall provoke a similar phenomenon ;
fermentation will set in and transform
the sugar into alcohol.   Barley, maize,
rice, molasses, beetroot, potatoes, and
practically all vegetal products, contain
either some sugar or some other
matter, such as starch, which can be
transformed into sugar ; they can be
thus caused to ferment, to yield some
alcohol, which may be separated later
by distillation.

Sugar-cane, molasses, beetroot and
those tubers, commonly called Jerusalem
artichokes, all contain a fairly large
proportion of sugar ; they have only
to be crushed or mashed and diluted ;
yeast is then added and they are thus
fermented in a direct way.

Wheat, barley, rye, oats, maize and
rice contain no sugar, but starch in
varying porportions, and by malting,
starch is transformed into glucose ;
yeast will cause the glucose to ferment,
and alcohol is thus obtained.

In a ·similar way, the starch contained

in potatoes is transformed into glucose, which, by the addition of yeast, is caused to ferment and to produce alcohol.

Having obtained by fermentation an alcoholic liquid, it only remains to distil it.

Different elements are affected differently by heat. The heat, for instance, which will melt butter, will not melt lead, and the heat which will suffice to melt lead, will not melt copper; if one had, for instance, a piece of mineral composed of lead and copper, one could separate them by heat, because the lead would melt first.

In the same way, the boiling point of water being 100° Centigrade, if one were to heat some sea water to 100°, the water would be vaporised, that is to say, it would become vapour—or steam— but the salt contained in the water would remain intact because salt only vaporises at a temperature of 1,000°.

In the same way, heat vaporises alcohol at a temperature of 78° Centigrade ; so that if we put in a saucepan

some wine or any other alcoholic liquid
and place it on the fire, vapours of alcohol should be obtained as soon as the
liquid reaches 78° and no water vapours
should be emitted, if we are careful not
to allow the temperature of the liquid
to reach 100°.

If this were the case, distillation
would be very much simpler than it is ;
but it is not so, because such an affinity
exists between alcohol and water, that
it is very difficult to separate the one
from the other at any given temperature.

Pure alcohol (anhydre) will be vaporised at 78°, but a temperature of 83·1
is required to vaporise an alcoholic liquid
containing 50 per cent. of alcohol and
50 per cent. of water ; and, if an
alcoholic liquid, such as wine, contained
only 10 per cent. of alcohol, a temperature
of 92·6 would be required to vaporise
the said liquid ; 92·6 is very near the
100° when all the water is bound to come
also.

The vapours which are emitted by
the wine placed in the saucepan will

therefore contain both water and alcohol, although more of the latter and less of the former than originally.

If we now put a lid on that saucepan, the steam or vapour will at once be condensed into a great number of small drops which will adhere to the cold surface of the lid and we can cause them to run into a glass. The alcoholic liquid we have thus obtained, first by vaporisation and then by condensation, still contains a large proportion of water, but being placed over the fire once more it will again emit vapours which we shall condense again, and which will contain a greater proportion of alcohol than before, but too much water still. We can then do the same thing, again and again, further rectifying our spirit, until we have reduced the proportion of water as much as we wish or can.

Distillation, therefore, may be said to necessitate three distinct essential operations :

Firstly :   VAPORISATION, to produce alcoholic vapours.

Secondly: CONDENSATION, to collect the said vapours.

Thirdly: RECTIFICATION, to free the said vapours from any excess of water or other matters which they may contain.

These three principal operations are quite distinct from each other in theory, but not always so in practice.

We must remember that, although pure alcohol becomes vaporised at a temperature of 78°, the boiling point of water is 100°, and that the greater therefore the proportion of water in any alcoholic liquid, the greater will have to be the heat to vaporise the alcohol, according to the following scale:

% of Alcohol.		% of Water.		Boiling point.	
.100	-	0	-	78°	Centigrade.
90	-	10	-	78°·8	,,
80	-	20	-	79°·7	,,
70	-	30	-	80°·9	,,
60	-	40	-	81°·9	,,
50	-	50	-	83°·1	,,
40	-	60	-	84°·1	,,
20	-	80	-	88°·3	,,
10	-	90	-	92°·6	,,
1	-	99	-	99°·06	,,
0	-	100	-	100°	,,

Bearing this in mind, let us take a

glass vessel composed of a chamber to contain the liquid we wish to distil, and fitted at the top with a pipe or tube to lead off the vapours into a receptacle placed at the end of it; we shall then have a still in its simplest form, but a still all the same. If we fill our still with some alcoholic liquid containing, for instance, 20 per cent. of alcohol, and place it over a fire, as soon as the temperature of the liquid reaches 88°·3, vapours of alcohol will be produced which will go up the tube, but which will be followed by water vapours. The vapours which reach the tube will contain a greater proportion of alcohol than the liquid they came from; and if they contain 40 per cent. of alcohol instead of 20 per cent., the alcohol they hold will be vaporised at 84°·1. When they have travelled some way along the glass tube, they are further from the fire, and the temperature of the lower part of the tube will probably be four degrees cooler than that of the mass of the liquid. As a temperature of 84°·1 is sufficient to vaporise

alcohol, the alcohol contained in the
vapours which have come from the
mass of the liquid, will still remain
vaporised, and will go further up the
tube ; but the water present in the same
vapours will find it too cold to remain
vaporised, and a good deal of it will be
condensed into water again, and fall
back into the mass of the liquid whence
it originally came. So that when the
vapours reach the top of the tube, they
contain a greater proportion of alcohol
than when they first entered it. They
may then contain 50 per cent. of alcohol,
and we know that, in that proportion, the
alcohol will be vaporised at a temperature of $83°·1$; on the other hand, the
top of the tube, being further away still
from the fire, will probably be one degree
cooler than the lower part, and the same
phenomenon will repeat itself ; some
more of the water contained in the vapours will be condensed at the lower temperature, and will fall back into the liquid
it came from, whilst the alcohol will still
be vaporised, and will pass on further
in the shape of alcoholic vapours into

a receptacle where the temperature
must always be kept well below 78°,
so that, even if vapours of pure alcohol
entered, they would be condensed
immediately.

Now, if this pipe or tube through
which the alcoholic vapours have to
travel were long enough; if it could be
separated inside in a series of compart-
ments; if the temperature of each com-
partment could be regulated and graduated
from 100°, the boiling point of water,
down to 78°, the boiling point of alcohol, we should be able, theoretically, to
isolate from any alcoholic liquid all the
alcohol it contained.

In practice, however, this is not
possible, and, in most cases it is not
even desirable, since the object of distillation, when applied to potable spirits,
is not to separate all or nearly all the
alcohol contained in any alcoholic liquid
from all the water, ethers, essential oils,
and other matters of which the said liquid
is composed.

A light white wine and strong beer,
for instance, are very different alcoholic

liquids, although both contain some ethyl alcohol. If both wine and beer could be distilled, rectified and redistilled until all the ethyl alcohol contained in each had been completely isolated, the spirit obtained would be identical in each case ; it would be simply plain spirit or pure spirit, plain or pure because it would be free from all such by-products as are always contained in grape juice or malted barley.

On the other hand, the object of distillation being principally to reduce the proportion of water contained in such liquids, if both wine and beer have been caused to contain each 50 per cent. of alcohol, the result will be a grape spirit and a grain spirit as distinct as the wine and beer they have been distilled from. The alcohol, from a chemical standpoint, will be the same in each case but the by-products or impurities will be very different, and it is these by-products which are responsible for the distinctiveness of all spirits other than highly rectified spirits, which should contain none.

In other words,. it may be asserted

that the quality and distinctiveness of
spirits vary according to the nature
and proportion of the by-products they
contain, and not owing to any differences in the chemical composition of
their alcohol.

Wine distilled until it contained 99
per cent. of ethyl alcohol would be purer
as spirit, but worse as Brandy, than
wine distilled only to 50 per cent.
On the other hand, a liquid fermented
from potatoes, if distilled to 50 per cent.,
would be 49 per cent. worse, as well as
less pure, than a spirit obtained from
the same liquid distilled to 99 per
cent.

In all alcoholic liquids, the ethers,
essential oils, acidity, mineral matters,
and other component parts, vary greatly,
some being retained with advantage after
distillation, whilst others must be elimin-
ated altogether.

The nature and proportion of the by-
products contained in different spirits
vary considerably, according to two main
causes :—

1°. According to the nature of the

alcoholic liquids from which
different spirits are distilled.

2°. According to the strength at
which spirits are distilled,
and according to different
methods of distillation.

Taking, for example, a mash made
from malted barley, if we distil part of
it until it contains 50 per cent. of alcohol, and if we distil another part further
until it contains 90 per cent. of alcohol,
we may then add to the latter some
water and thus reduce it to 50 per cent.
of alcohol, or in other words, to proof;
the two spirits will then contain the
same percentage of alcohol, but they
will differ considerably in every other
respect, because the first will possess
a much larger proportion of the distinctive by-products of the malted
barley from which it was distilled.

CHAPTER VI

Alcohol and the Human Body

IT is one of Nature's own laws to render agreeable that which is useful and the natural liking for alcohol amongst all races and in all times is a proof in itself that alcohol is intended by Nature for the use and for the good of mankind.

As far back as we can go in the annals of the world's history, we find abundant and undeniable proofs of the constant use and abuse of alcohol. It would be strange, indeed, if the instinct of so many generations should have been at fault during all the past centuries of which we possess documentary evidence; and it would be stranger still if alcohol were otherwise than beneficial to both body and mind when, at the present moment, we are bound to acknowledge that all Great Powers are the least abstemious nations ; furthermore, it may be rightly asserted that the consumption of alcoholic beverages is greater in those countries which are the most prosperous or the most highly civilised, whilst Buddhists and Moslems, who excelled in all arts and were races of rulers before they had become water-drinkers, are now either under the rule or at the mercy of alcohol-drinking races.

History and common sense supply us with a mass of evidence in favour of the beneficial effects of alcohol upon the human body, but it is highly interesting to know whether and in what degree their verdict is endorsed by modern science ; let us, therefore, put aside historical proofs and all circumstantial evidence, and let us examine the question from a purely scientific point of view.

The only scientific and rational manner of approaching the question is, first of all, to know what is meant by the word alcohol.

Alcohol is the name of a class of neutral compounds of carbon, hydrogen and oxygen, capable of forming ethers with acids. This class comprises a great many members, some of which, far from being volatile, are not even liquid. Cetyl alcohol, for instance, is a solid fat whilst cerylic and myricylic alcohols are waxy. Glycerine, which is a trihydric or triatomic alcohol ($C_3H_8O_3$), fusel oil or amylic alcohol ($C_5H_{12}O$), methyl alcohol (CH_4O), propyl alcohol (C_3H_8O), butylic alcohol ($C_4H_{10}O$) and a great many more, all have an equal right to the name alcohol. But, by far the most important member of this large family is ethylic alcohol (C_2H_6O), a compound of two molecules of carbon, six of hydrogen and one of oxygen. In other words, ethylic alcohol has the same chemical composition as water with one of its hydrogen atoms replaced by a hydro-carbon radical composed of two atoms of carbon and five of hydrogen.

Scientifically speaking, the term alcohol should always be qualified, but, when used alone, it is understood to refer to ethylic alcohol, the principal stimulating agent of all alcoholic beverages.

The chemical composition of ethylic alcohol is beyond controversy and there is absolutely nothing in the chemical composition of ethylic alcohol which would entitle it to be called a poison or a narcotic ; it has none of the chemical characteristics of known poisons, and it does not possess any of their properties.

Alcohol is a nutrient and a nervine ; that is to say, a food with a specific action upon the nervous system.

Alcohol, like carbo-hydrates, such as sugar, creates heat and furnishes energy for muscular work.

Alcohol has a specific action upon the nervous system ; an action which leads to perfectly normal functional changes, and causes a certain inner mental stimulation.

The Food Value of Alcohol

The two functions of food are to furnish materials for the formation of

M

the tissues of the body, and to yield
energy for warmth and for muscular
work. Nitrogenous foods or proteids,
such as the casein of milk, the albumen
of egg, the gluten of wheat, etc., are
tissue-building foods, whilst fats, such
as butter, and carbo-hydrates, such as
sugar or starch, supply the energy or
fuel required ; they are burned, or
oxidised, and transformed into heat
and muscular strength. Alcohol contains no nitrogen and, therefore, cannot
build tissue, any more than sugar or
starch can, but it is a food in the same
sense as these, supplying heat and
energy by oxidation in the body.

That alcohol is almost entirely
oxidised in the body, except when
taken in very large quantities, has
been proved by the most exhaustive
scientific experiments. " The outcome
of the best investigation on this subject may be summarised as follows,"
writes Professor W. O. Atwater, " The
alcohol of ordinary beverages is easily
absorbed from the stomach and the
intestines into the circulation, and

readily burned. If the amount taken is small, the oxidation is almost complete. When the quantity taken is excessive, the amount unconsumed is likely to be much larger. As the experiments with alcohol have been more accurate, the proportion actually oxidised has appeared larger and larger. When taken in small quantities—say, one or two glasses of wine or a glass of whisky at a time—the alcohol has been found to be burned at least as completely as bread or meat. The reason for discussing at such a length a theory discarded a quarter of a century ago by the leading authorities is that it has remained current in the writings of some authors, and even in some of our school text-books which deny the food value of alcohol."

The oxidation of alcohol in the body is a fact placed by science beyond all doubt, but it is far more difficult to ascertain the amount of heat and energy produced by the oxidation of alcohol, and, therefore, the actual food value of alcohol.

To compare the degree of nourishing power of different foods, we must remember that the caloric or heat-power of different substances differs, that is to say that the heat and energy which will be produced by the oxidation of one ounce of sugar, for instance, will differ from the heat and energy which the oxidation of one ounce of butter will produce. Very exhaustive experiments were carried out by Professor Atwater and the *Committee of Fifty for the investigation of the liquor problem* which was appointed by the United States Government some few years ago, for the purpose of ascertaining the food value of alcohol. Pure ethylic alcohol, diluted in water or coffee, was used for these experiments, and it is claimed that when the quantity of fat, sugar and starch was reduced by what would produce 500 caloric units and replaced by a sufficient quantity of alcohol to furnish 500 caloric units, the work done and the energy given off from the body were practically the same. This proved that alcohol not only was oxidised in the body but also to the same good purpose as a similar heat giving quantity of fat, sugar and starch ; in other words, alcohol supplied the same energy to the body as fats and carbo-hydrates. Furthermore, it was proved in the most absolute manner that, when carbo-hydrates were replaced by alcohol, in the diet of the subject experimented upon, there was no need to increase the proportion of albumin included in the diet ; alcohol acted in exactly the same way as carbo-hydrates in saving the albumin stored in the body, an absolute proof of its being a nutrient.

Further evidence of the food value of alcohol has been provided by many scientific experiments made to test the influence of alcohol on muscular effort and fatigue, the favourite method employed for these experiments being the use of the ergograph.

The ergograph is an instrument designed to register the variations of muscular effort ; it is derived from two Greek words, *ergon* which means work, and *graphein*, to write. Either the middle finger or the last joint of that finger is fitted with a ring of leather to which is attached by a string a weight of about nine pounds hanging over a pulley; the forearm and hand being at rest, this one finger is bent at fixed intervals in rapid succession, the weight being lifted as high as possible until exhaustion occurs. By an ingenious contrivance, a needle is fixed to the apparatus which traces a curve indicating the rapidity of the contractions and the height to which the weight is lifted each time.

The first worker to use the ergograph for the investigation of the action of alcohol was W. P. Lombard in 1892; taking small doses of alcohol, in the form of Claret, he found an increase in the amount of work, the effect showing itself in a few minutes, and lasting in one case for an hour-and-a-half. Two years later, Rossi tested the action of alcohol, in the form of rum, on the work executed in fifteen ergograms, taken at intervals of ten minutes. With doses of eighty grammes, corresponding probably to about thirty grammes of absolute alcohol, he found an increase in the total amount of work, but this increase was chiefly due to the earlier ergograms, the latter showing a decrease as compared with the work of days on which no alcohol had been taken. With smaller doses of twenty-five grammes of rum, the favourable influence was more pronounced, and persisted for the whole of the two hours during which the experiment lasted.

Frey, whose work was published in 1896, found that the action of alcohol on the fatigued muscle was different from that on the unfatigued muscle. When alcohol was given ten minutes before beginning to work with the ergograph, the effect in most persons was to diminish the amount of work. If, on the other hand, the alcohol was given after a certain number of ergograms had been recorded, so that some fatigue had been induced, Frey found that alcohol had a beneficial effect, and that the increase in the amount of work might be considerable. From these observations, he concluded that alcohol has a double action—an injurious action on the nervous system, which predominates when the muscle is unfatigued, and a beneficial action as a food for the muscle substance.

In 1897, was published a paper by Tavernari, who found that 50 grammes of Marsala Wine, taken after a fairly long walk, doubled the amount of work executed with the ergograph.

In 1899, the observations recorded by Kraepelin and based chiefly on Gluck's work, were published. Two series of observations, each of eight days, were made, the first with pauses of 10 minutes and the second with pauses of 3 minutes between the ergograms. The alcohol was given not in wine, beer or spirits, but in the form of ethylic alcohol in doses of 40 grammes, a very hard test indeed as regards both the nature and the amount of alcohol taken. In the first series, with pauses of ten minutes, there was a marked initial increase, which disappeared to a large extent in the second ergogram, but the work remained above the average during the whole duration of the experiment until the last curve, which showed a slight sinking below the level of the days on which no alcohol had been taken ; the whole work, however, showed an increase of 13 per cent. above that of the " non-alcohol days." In the second series, with pauses of only three minutes, the effect was different ; there was a large initial increase of 30 per cent. which disappeared in the second ergogram, from which point there was a diminution in the amount of work, so that at the end the total work was only half that of the " non-alcohol days."

In the same year, Schumburg published some observations on the effect of alcohol, in which he claims that, in uncomplicated ergographic work, alcohol had a beneficial influence, but that in the presence of general fatigue produced by work with the ergostat, it had no influence.

In 1900, appeared the work of Scheffer

who experimented upon himself and
used Mosso's ergograph. Ten grammes
of absolute alcohol were taken immediately in one series, and fifteen minutes
before the beginning of the work in
another, and in each case the amount
of work was increased. In a third series
in which the same dose was taken
thirty minutes before beginning to work,
the effect was unfavourable, a smaller
amount of work being done with alcohol
throughout.

In 1901, an account of the work done
by Oseretzkowsky and Kraepelin was
published; ergograms were taken at two
minutes' intervals, and, after the seventh,
a dose of alcohol was taken, and the
work was continued for an hour. The
alcohol was only taken on four days, fifteen
grammes being taken twice, and thirty
and fifty grammes respectively on the
other two days. On one day the dose
of fifteen grammes produced an increase,
which continued to the end of the experiment; on the other day, there was
a slight falling off as compared with
the average of three days on which no

alcohol was taken. The doses of thirty and fifty grammes produced very little effect. In the same Paper, there are also recorded experiments by Moskiewicz with a dose of thirty grammes taken during three days, which showed a slight increase on the alcohol days.

In 1903, Schnyder published an interesting Paper, in which he gives evidence that the effect of alcohol may be different according as it is taken soon after a meal or at a considerable interval. His first observations were made four hours after a meal, six to twelve ergograms being recorded at minute intervals. The alcohol was taken in the form of Claret and in such an amount that the dose of absolute alcohol would be about fifteen grammes. In one series, the alcohol was taken fifteen minutes before beginning to work by two subjects, and in both cases there was an increase in the total amount of work, equal to ten per cent. in one case, and to five per cent. in the other. In the second set of experiments, Schnyder tried the effect of thirty grammes doses of alcohol taken during a meal and found that, in both subjects, there was a slight decrease in the total amount of work.

In 1904, the "Travaux du Laboratoire de Physiologie" published Mdlle. Joteyko's interesting work on alcohol. She generally used small doses of alcohol (twenty grammes), and found very great individual differences among the seven persons who were experimented upon. Three were almost entirely resistant to the action of alcohol, even when the dose was increased to fifty grammes, though two then showed a slight diminution in the amount of work. Two other persons showed a decided increase in the amount of work after doses of twenty to thirty grammes of alcohol. The remaining two subjects showed a decided diminution—in one case even with ten grammes of alcohol—and this action was so pronounced in one case that the weight could hardly be lifted at all after twenty grammes of alcohol had been taken.

In 1908, Rivers experimented upon himself and a friend, Mr. Webber, a life-long abstainer and temperance worker. The most interesting part of River's experiments is that he states that when comparatively small doses of ethylic alcohol were taken, the work suffered, whilst after forty c.c. of whisky, in Webber's case, and two glasses of champagne in his own case, there was a very marked increase in the amount of ergographic work they were able to do.

The fact that alcohol is a food and is oxidised in the body like carbohydrates, such as sugar or starch, is only too often overlooked, and alcohol then becomes a danger. Corpulence, gout, dilatation or relaxation of the heart, and similar diseases, are more frequent amongst drinkers than abstainers, but it is scientifically wrong to blame alcohol for any such complaints ; they are solely due to over-nutrition, not to alcohol as such. People who eat as much proteids, fats and carbo-hydrates as they require, and even more than they require, and at the same time do not deny themselves the pleasure and comfort of alcoholic beverages, should realise that by so doing they are taking more food in the shape of alcohol, and an excess of food which must perforcedly be injurious to the body. Alcoholic beverages should be taken in place of, and not in addition to, a certain amount of fats and carbo-hydrates; if the body is supplied with all the fats and carbo-hydrates required to produce the necessary heat and energy, alcohol will only cause fat deposits in organs in which fat cannot be used.

It might be said that, since alcohol takes the place of carbo-hydrates, carbo-hydrates could also take the place of alcohol, so that by increasing the proportion of fats or carbo-hydrates in one's diet, one might easily dispense with alcohol.

If alcohol were nothing but a food, this assumption would be quite correct, but it is absolutely incorrect because alcohol is not only a food, but a food with a very marked specific action upon the nervous system. As a nutrient, alcohol can be replaced by carbo-hydrates, but as a nervine it has no substitute. Most people drink alcoholic beverages for the specific action they exercise upon the nervous system and the brain, but many fail to realise that alcohol also possesses a very real food value which is beneficial in itself but becomes a serious danger, as in the case of all foods, when taken in excess.

The Specific Action of Alcohol upon the Nervous System and the Brain

Our nervous system is the most complicated part of our organism. It comprises a central nervous system, including the brain and spinal cord, and, leading from these, a network of nerves controlling all the organs and glands of the body.

We know that alcohol excites in a specific manner the sensory nerves of smell and taste, since we can easily detect its presence whenever we are either smelling or tasting it. We also know that alcohol has a marked action upon the secreting nerves of glands, which it causes to contract and discharge their cell contents, saliva in the mouth or gastric juices in the stomach. This is the result of perfectly normal functional changes which have nothing in common with disturbances.

As soon as alcohol comes into contact with the mucuous membrane of the stomach, a more abundant but perfectly normal secretion of gastric juices takes place as a result of the excitation or contraction of the nervous end-apparatus of the stomach.

To ascertain experimentally the action of alcohol upon the nervous system, and particularly so upon the brain or central nervous system, is as yet beyond the reach of science.

Professor Kraepelin and his pupils of the Heidelberg School have, it is true, investigated the action of alcohol on the mental processes. The methods they employed consisted chiefly in ascertaining the speed and character of various mental exercises, and then observing how far they are modified by the administration to the subject under examination of various doses of alcohol. The experiments were devised principally to estimate the acuteness of perception as shown, for instance, by the recognition of letters, syllables or figures presented to the sight for very brief periods ; and to demonstrate the rapidity and accuracy displayed in such exercises as reading aloud, adding rows of figures, committing figures to memory, etc.

The inherent vice of all such experiments is that they are carried out under conditions which greatly differ from those of ordinary life. The subjects who are asked to produce certain mental efforts before, during or after being given to drink various doses of alcohol, are bound to be influenced to a large extent by the mere knowledge of what is expected of them. Besides, it is universally recognised that alcohol, like shellfish, milk, fruit, and all aliments, will affect different men differently, and also that any one man may be affected differently by the same quantity of alcohol, taken in the shape of either wine, beer or spirits. It is quite easy to understand that a German compositor, for instance, who usually drinks German beer, is not likely to set up type at a quicker rate when treated by the experimenting professor to some " Greek wine " or to some German brandy distilled from potatoes and diluted in coffee ;

N

the quantity of ethylic alcohol may be
the same, but everything else is so different that whatever phenomenon may be
observed as a result of the change of diet
cannot scientifically be attributed to alcohol.

This is why Dr. W. C. Sullivan, Medical Officer in His Majesty's Prison Service,
and one of the most conscientious temperance advocates of the present day,
when dealing with the experimental
methods applied to the study of the influence of alcohol upon the nervous system,
wrote : " Of course, it will readily be
understood that the conclusions to which
this sort of evidence can lead are for the
most part merely probable. The questions
at issue are of such complexity that it is
very difficult to devise experiments for
their solution that will not be open to
many and grave fallacies ; the effects
of slight differences in technique or of
peculiarities in individual reaction are
likely to show on an exaggerated scale,
and hence to produce discordant results ;
and even when the results are agreed on,
their interpretation will still depend upon
physiological principles regarding which

the sharpest and most radical differences of opinion prevail."

Although it is not possible to gauge experimentally the action of alcohol upon the nervous system with any degree of scientific accuracy, it has been abundantly proved by medical experiments and every day experience that alcohol has a marked specific action upon the creative faculties of the brain.

The human brain possesses both active and passive properties; imagination, for instance, is one of the active or creative faculties, whilst memory is simply passive or receptive. The passive and active faculties of the brain are quite distinct. Many animals possess a receptive brain; their sense of locality, their memory and their instinct guide them, but they are incapable of original thought, imaginative power, or high ideals. On the other hand, men of real genius, who have attained to great celebrity in the world of letters, arts, or politics, have been known to lack memory and the instinct of self-preservation, which even the lower animals possess.

Alcohol has the very remarkable pro-
perty of deadening to a certain extent
the passive or receptive faculties of the
brain whilst exciting and stimulating, at
the same time, its active or creative powers
and the inner self or personal psychic ego
of man.

Alcohol cannot supply brain power
where there is none nor make a selfish
man unselfish or a fool clever. It will,
however, bring into play, stimulate into
action, and intensify the temperament
and the qualities, good, bad or indifferent,
it may be one's good or bad fortune to
possess.

Alcohol will help the poet, the artist,
the orator, to forget the petty cares and
troubles which may harass him ; it will
deaden the sense of self-consciousness
and diffidence which drove him to sterile
inaction, and, at the same time, it will
stimulate his genius to greater activity.
But alcohol will only cause the sanguine
and brainless man to be jolly, the bilious
fool to be irritable and the phlegmatic
dullard to be peacefully happy ; it can
never create sense where there is none.

In other words alcohol urges the gifted to remember and use their gifts and hides from the giftless the injustice of fate.

Doctor Charles Mercier, in his *Inaugural Address on Drunkenness and the physiological effect of Alcohol*, delivered before the Midland Medical Association, in November, 1912, expressed the same truths in a more scientific manner, when he said : " Alcohol has the power to unlock the store of energy that exists in the brain, and to render available, for immediate expenditure, energy that without its use would remain in store, unavailable for our immediate needs."

The Use and Abuse of Alcohol

Ethylic alcohol is a food with a specific action upon the nervous system, and this fact not only justifies the use of alcoholic beverages but it also explains scientifically why they have been used in all ages and amongst all civilised nations.

Excellent as the moderate use of alcohol is, its abuse cannot be too

strongly deprecated. In all questions of
diet, moderation is a golden rule which
can never be broken without grave danger.
All aliments become a source of danger
—and will even become poison—above
a certain dose. Daily excessive ingestion
of any fluid must burden the heart, the
blood vessels and the kidneys ; whether
the liquid ingested be water, milk or beer,
the difference will be one of degree, not
of kind ; excessive drinking of water is
bad, but excessive drinking of milk or
beer is worse, because of their food value.
What is known as the beer-heart, for
instance, is not the result of the action
of alcohol, but of over-nutrition ; it is
the abnormal quantities of liquid, and
not the small percentage of alcohol contained therein, which have overtaxed the
functions of the heart and caused the
fatty degenerescence of that organ.

It must be remembered that although
they all contain a certain proportion
of ethylic alcohol, all alcoholic beverages vary considerably on account of the
different elements they are composed of,
far more than on account of the more

or less important quantity of ethylic
alcohol they may contain. There might
be, for instance, exactly the same quantity
of ethylic alcohol in a pint of light Moselle
as in a glass of beer ; in a pint of Claret
as in a glass of Port ; in two glasses of
Champagne as in one glass of whisky
and soda ; in a glass of brandy as in a
glass of gin ; but, in each case, different
physiological results are likely to be obtained. Just as one man cannot eat beef
but enjoys mutton, as another who
cannot digest cabbage will eat celery with
impunity, or as another for whom strawberries are a poison yet may eat pine-
apple, so there are people whom beer
suits better than wine or *vice versâ* ;
brandy may suit one man better than
whisky, whilst the reverse happens to
be the case with another. It is true
that the chemical nature of the ethylic
alcohol is identical in both wine and beer,
but the many other elements of which
beer and wine are composed are altogether
different, and they cannot be equally
suitable in all cases.

Ethylic alcohol is of considerable value

to the economy of our organism, but
it should never be abused nor taken in
the shape of one or the other alcoholic
beverages which may not be suitable to
individual temperaments or in particular
cases. He who suffers from diabetes,
for instance, must not blame alcohol if
he finds that the sweet wine he drinks
disagrees with him; let him take the
same moderate quantity of alcohol in
the shape of dry and somewhat acid
wines and he will find that they suit
him admirably. Just as sugar is to be
avoided in cases of diabetes or asparagus
in kidney diseases, so should alcohol be
avoided in all complaints when in-
flammation or fever occurs. But, with
that exception, the number and variety
of alcoholic beverages are so great, that
in health and sickness, in youth and
old age, bountiful Nature has provided
for us a marvellously ordained range of
wholesome stimulants to suit all different
temperaments, tastes and circumstances.

Like most of God's best gifts, alcohol
always has been and still is abused. The
sin of drunkenness has been justly

denounced in Holy Writ, as well as by all the philosophers of ancient Greece and Rome and by all moralists ever since. It was not, however, until the last century that some men in this country revived Mahommed's heresy and preached the doctrine of total abstinence.

Amongst those who to-day share the new faith, there are men who have attained to such eminence in the medical profession, that we are bound to ask ourselves how and why it is that such great intellects should have adopted views in utter contradiction to the universal experience of mankind and experimental science.

It certainly seems strange that one of the ablest of our London specialists should affix his name to a book purporting to prove scientifically that alcohol is a poison, at all times injurious to body and mind alike, and to find that the scientific proofs of this statement are based on experiments made with jelly-fish, water-fleas, water-cress, etc., showing that the lowest forms of animal and plant life are injuriously affected by the

action of alcohol, just as if jelly-fish would
not equally resent being placed in milk,
however rich in cream, or even in distilled water. Another suggested experiment in the same book is to drop some
brandy into the naked eye and realise
the disturbance caused by the " poison."
Further, the few unfavourable reports of
investigators with the ergograph are also
given, but all the favourable results obtained by the same and other investigators
are carefully omitted.

It would be unjust to those doctors who
advocate total abstinence to believe them
capable of looking on such so called proofs
as scientific. It is not science, it is not
common sense, it is not truth on which
stands their faith in water ; it is their
charity, their pity for the poor deserted
children of the drunkard, the hapless
young wife of the dipsomaniac. They
see the evils—evils which are real and
great—which are due to the *abuse* of
alcohol, and they are so moved by the
bodily and mental misery which they
have personally known to be caused by
such abuse, that they lose sight of the

fact that the benefits accruing from the proper use of alcohol are far greater than the evils due to its abuse ; they forget what they often owe themselves to the moderate use of stimulants, and what the world, what their own country owes to alcohol. They forget that from Chaucer, the son of a royal butler, to Ruskin, the son and grandson of wine merchants, every poet, dramatist, artist and writer of genius, every great thinker has been a wine drinker ; that every ruler, every prime minister, every brain-worker, who has ever merited his country's and perchance humanity's gratitude, all have used and some have abused that most noble gift of a divine Providence : Wine.

EXTRACT FROM THE " LANCET."

MARCH 30TH, 1907.

In view of the statement frequently made as to present Medical opinion regarding alcohol and alcoholic beverages, we, the undersigned, think it desirable to issue the following short statement on the subject—a statement which, we believe, represents the opinions of the leading Clinical Teachers, as well as of the great majority of Medical practitioners.

Recognising that, in prescribing alcohol, the requirements of the individual must be the governing rule, we are convinced of the correctness of the opinion so long and generally held, that in disease alcohol is a rapid and trustworthy restorative. In many cases it may be truly described as life-preserving, owing to its power to sustain cardiac and nervous energy, while protecting the wasting nitrogenous tissues.

As an article of diet we hold that the universal belief of civilised mankind that the moderate use of alcoholic beverages, is, for adults, usually beneficial, is amply justified.

We deplore the evils arising from the abuse of alcoholic beverages. But it is obvious that there is nothing, however, beneficial, which does not by excess become injurious.

> T. McCALL ANDERSON, M.D., Regius Professor of Medicine, University of Glasgow.
> ALFRED G. BARRS.
> WILLIAM H. BENNETT, K.C.V.O., F.R.C.S.
> JAMES CRICHTON-BROWNE.
> W. E. DIXON.

DYCE DUCKWORTH, M.D., LL.D.
THOMAS R. FRASER, M.D., F.R.S.
T. R. GLYNN.
W. R. GOWERS, M.D., F.R.S.
W. D. HALLIBURTON, M.D., LL.D., F.R.C.P.,
    F.R.S., Professor of Physiology, King's
    College, London.
JONATHAN HUTCHINSON.
ROBERT HUTCHISON.
EDMUND OWEN, LL.D., F.R.C.S.
P. H. PYE-SMITH.
FRED. T. ROBERTS, M.D. B.Sc., F.R.C.P.
EDGCOMBE VENNING, F.R.C.S.

Extract from the "Lancet."

November 30th, 1912.

. . . In further corroboration of my thesis that
the effect of moderate doses of alcohol is to stimulate
the mental faculties of those who possess mental
faculties, and stimulate those faculties which some
think the highest, such as imagination, fancy, picturesque imagery—the artistic faculties as we may call
them—I point to the fact that there has never been
one distinguished originator in any branch of art
who did not take alcohol, at least in moderation, and
many have taken it, alas! in excess. It is the fact,
indisputable if lamentable, that it is the great nations,
the victorious nations, the progressive nations, the
nations that are in the van of civilisation, that are

the drinking nations. I don't say they are great because they drink, but I do say that this disposes of the argument that a drinking nation is necessarily a decadent nation.

A world of total abstainers might be a decorous world, a virtuous world, a world perhaps a little too conscious of its own merits ; but there is no reason to suppose that it would be an uncontentious or un-prejudiced world, or a world from which exaggera-tion of statement, intemperance in speech, or intoler-ance of opinion would be banished ; and there is some evidence to make us anxious lest it should be a drab, inartistic, undecorated world ; a world without poetry, without music, without painting, without romance ; utterly destitute of humour ; taking sadly what pleasures it allowed itself ; and rather priding itself on its indifference to the charms of wine, woman, and song. . . .

(Extract from the *Inaugural Address on Drunken-ness and the Physiological Effect of Alcohol*, delivered before the Midland Medical Society, by Charles Mercier, M.D., F.R.C.P.)

Wyman & Sons Ltd., Printers, London and Reading.

CPSIA information can be obtained at www.ICGtesting.com
Printed in the USA
LVOW10*1505150415

434707LV00005B/86/P

9 781163 841907